COMPUTERS
AND
TYPOGRAPHY

POLIPHILO INCOMINCIA IL SECONDO LIBRO DI
LA SVA HYPNEROTOMACHIA. NEL QVALE PO-
LIA ET LVI DISERTABONDI, IN QVALE MODO ET
VARIO CASO NARRANO INTERCALARIAMEN-
TE IL SVO INAMORAMENTO.

NARRA QVIVI LA DIVA POLIA LA NOBILE ET
ANTIQVA ORIGINE SVA. ET COMO PER LI PREDE
CESSORI SVI TRIVISIO FVE EDIFICATO. ET DI QVEL
LA GENTE LELIA ORIVNDA. ET PER QVALE MO-
DO DISAVEDVTA ET INSCIA DISCONCIAMENTE
SE INAMOROE DI LEI IL SVO DILECTO POLIPHILO.

E MIE DEBILE VOCE TALE O GRA
tiose & diue Nymphe abfone peruenerano &
inconcine alla uoftra benigna audietia, quale
la terrifica raucitate del urinante Efacho al fua-
ue canto dela piangeuole Philomela. Nondi
meno uolendo io cum tuti gli mei exili conati del intellecto, & cum la mia paucula fufficie
tia di fatiffare alle uoftre piaceuole petitione,
non riftaro al potere. Lequale femota qualuque hefitatione epfe piu che
fi congruerebbe altronde, dignamente meritano piu uberrimo fluuio di
eloquentia, cum troppo piu rotunda elegantia & cum piu exornata poli
tura di pronutiato, che in me per alcuno pacto non fi troua, di cofeguire
il fuo gratiofo affecto. Ma a uui Celibe Nymphe & adme alquato, quan
tuche & confufa & incomptamete fringultiete haro in qualche portiun-
cula gratificato affai. Quando uoluntarofa & diuota a gli defii uoftri &
poftulato me preftaro piu prefto cum lanimo no mediocre prompto hu-
mile parendo, che cum enucleata terfa, & uenufta eloquentia placedo. La
prifca dunque & ueterrima geneologia, & profapia, & il fatale mio amore
garrulando ordire. Onde gia effendo nel uoftro uenerando conuentuale
confpecto, & uederme fterile & ieiuna di eloquio & ad tanto preftate & di
uo ceto di uui O Nymphe fedule famularie dil accefo cupidine. Et itan-
to benigno & delecteuole & facro fito, di fincere aure & florigeri fpirami-
ni afflato. Io acconciamente compulfa di affumere uno uenerabile aufo,
& tranquillo timore de dire. Dunque auante il tuto uenia date, o belliffi-
me & beatiffime Nymphe a quefto mio blacterare & agli femelli & terri-
geni, & pufilluli Conati, fi aduene che in alchuna parte io incautamente

Page from the *Hypnerotomachia Poliphili*, Aldus Manutius, Venice 1499

COMPUTERS AND TYPOGRAPHY

Compiled by Rosemary Sassoon

The customary words 'edited by' have been omitted at my request. They might imply that I had some editorial say in each chapter, which I did not. I would be happy to put the phrase 'designed by' but that might be misinterpreted. I am a designer by training, not a typographer – so all I did was to design this book following my brief, then I appealed to my friends to help me carry it out. They are all specialists in one field or another. I shall always be grateful to them, and we are all indebted to Elwyn and Michael Blacker for the actual design of the book. It is an example of what this is all in aid of – typographic excellence in the computer age.

OXFORD, ENGLAND

First published in Great Britain in 1993 by
Intellect Books
Suite 2, 108/110 London Road, Oxford OX3 9AW

British Library Cataloguing in Publication data available

ISBN 1-871516-23-4

Publisher: Masoud Yazdani
Copy editor: Wendy Momen
Index: Roy Davies

Designed by Pardoe Blacker Publishing Limited
Shawlands Court, Newchapel Road, Lingfield, Surrey

Printed and bound in Great Britain by Bath Press, Bath

Contents

Preface

'We never realised that letterforms mattered'. This was the response to a poster display about typographic research at a conference for computer experts. It was that occasion which brought about the idea for this book. Its purpose is to bridge the gap between those in the field of computers and those concerned with typography. This set of papers sets out to raise awareness of the importance of letterforms and layout. It will not turn anyone into a typographer overnight, but it can start people noticing and then discriminating in such a way that we hope they will never again be satisfied with second best.

What is typography

It might be a good idea to define the word typography as it is used today. Fernand Baudin (1989) does this much better than I. In his book 'How Typography Works' he calls it 'the term we use to describe the process and appearance of typesetting'. He continues "The word Typographie to designate a printing shop was introduced in France as early as the mid-sixteenth century. Only in the late seventeenth century England did Typography begin to imply the theory of type design, type cutting, type casting, typesetting and printing. Today it tends to suggest the use of typefaces in communication generally.' Baudin, who I hope will not mind being called a typographic scholar, says something entirely relevant to this book when he writes, 'It even appears at times as if any computer-assisted keyboard gives direct access to the typographic heritage of five centuries. But this is only true as far as it goes. It is rather like saying that any piano gives direct access to the bulk of our musical heritage. To what extent this is true can be heard in the case of music as soon as anyone touches the keys of a piano. It can be seen in the case of typography whenever a keyboard operator is left on his or her own devices with a typographic problem to solve.'

One of the most complex problems concerns not the black letters but the white spaces. As Charles Bigelow (1985) explains, 'Lettering artists know that the "counters", the negative shapes of the background, are as important as the positive shapes of the letters. The relation between the form and the counter-form, between letters and their surroundings and internal spaces, is a crucial part of alphabet design ...The sizes and spacings of type are not arbitrary; they have been carefully tuned to the mechanisms of the visual system, not by rational analysis, but by centuries even millenia of careful scribal experimentation.'

Bridging the gap

This inter-disciplinary bridging must be done while there are still those about who were brought up in the traditions of typographic excellence who care enough and who are willing to share their knowledge. When I hesitantly approached a few of my busy friends for contributions, it soon became clear how strongly they all felt about passing on what they know to a new audience. There are relatively few of us who are actively involved in letterforms, whether those letters are written, drawn, cut by hand or computer-generated. We have been lucky to come from a long line of craftsmen whose tradition is to pass on all they know to the next generation. This book intends to make it apparent to all that the skill of manipulating letters is a vital one, not to be abandoned, not to be considered obsolete. It must be realized that letterforms are just as essential to modern technology as to traditional printing. Above all, the computer cannot be relied upon to make the vital qualitative judgements. The technologists must be aware of such matters and learn to apply this traditional knowledge in their work.

The best of our typographers have long become computer orientated in the traditions of their craft. Throughout the centuries they have adapted to changing technologies with barely a backward glance, adapting their accumulated knowledge to new developments in printing and communication. Most of us, however, are concerned that the study of letterforms has more or less disappeared from our schools and colleges. Children learn from an early age to call up characters on the screen, but even those who choose an art school training have missed out on the handling of letters, which is the best way of learning to discriminate. This has been going on for so long that right back in the chain of those who teach the teachers there is little knowlege or concern over something that is still a vital communication skill.

The authors of these papers have done a wonderful job, not only in a factual way, but in revealing their own feelings about letterforms. Maybe this is as good a way as any to lure others into the same frame of mind. Certainly such matters cannot be forced. It may not be easy to understand that letterforms can be as creative a means of expression as sculpture or painting. We all create our personal letterforms in our own handwriting. Understanding this is another route to appreciating letterforms, one that raises awareness of the fact that personal tastes and characteristics not only colour our handwritten letters but influence how we perceive other letterforms, even typefaces. This leads to the understanding that from type designers (sometimes a rather strong-minded lot) downwards, what suits one person may not always be suitable for the eyes and other specific needs of another particular set of readers.

This set of papers covers a wide variety of aspects about the relationship between computers and typography. The chapters range from invaluable practical advice to the historical and philosophical and the technical and research angles. It was not an easy job to divide the articles into categories. Some of us have strayed into each other's areas - but education and history cannot easily be separated, choice and criteria cannot be confined to the characters of only one writing system. Finally, to isolate research from its practical consequences seemed to diminish all that we stand for.

This book provides an open forum not only for disseminating information, but for much more. Every chapter raises issues that need to be discussed today in an informed manner. Our different disciplines cannot work together in a positive way if we do not understand the basis of each other's heritage and training. These are what form our attitudes and affect our priorities.

The authors' own words introduce each part of the book. They do it much better than I could. The wide-ranging bibliographies that they provide point to further reading for those who intend to delve deeper into the subject. Even so, it is only a beginning.

References

Baudin F. (1989). *How Typography Works (and Why it is Important)*. Lund Humphries.

Bigelow C. (1985). *Principles of Type Design for the Personal Workstation*. A keepsake prepared by Bigelow and Holmes for members at the ATypI Congress in Kiel.

PART I
SPACING AND LAYOUT

Introduction to text massage

GUNNLAUGUR SE BRIEM LETTERFORMS DESIGNER, CALIFORNIA, ENGLAND & ICELAND

There are, on the whole, two kinds of typographic masterpieces. One is bold and we admire it. The other is quiet and gets respect. What I tell you will give you a start on respect.

The layout of computer-based text

JAMES HARTLEY PSYCHOLOGIST AND RESEARCHER, KEELE UNIVERSITY, STAFFORDSHIRE. UK ST5 5BG

The overall size and orientation of the page or screen determines what can be presented to the reader. How one manipulates the space within this framework is important. Space can be systematically manipulated to show the structure of the text.

Presentation rules and rules of composition in the formatting of complex text

RICHARD SOUTHALL COMPUTER-TYPOGRAPHER AND RESEARCHER, 2 LONG ROW, WICKEN ROAD, LECKHAMPSTEAD, BUCKS. UK MK18 5NZ

The configuration of the actual document produced when a generically marked-up virtual document is formatted depends on *rules of composition* which govern the action of the formatting system, as well as on presentation rules associated with the document. Rules of composition are of two kinds: *spacing rules* and *rules of orthography*. Statements of such rules in compositors' manuals from the era of metal-type composition are quoted, and their underlying rationales discussed.

GUNNLAUGUR SE BRIEM

Introduction to text massage

What's 'text massage'? I'll tell you. You've set up a perfect framework for your piece: page numbers in place, margins and gutters neatly arranged. And when you dump the text into the columns, it looks like a dog's breakfast. You lead and kern. That's massage. You lift parentheses and throw in ligatures. After a while, you can have body text that is a work of art. That's massage.

There are, on the whole, two kinds of typographic masterpieces. One is bold, and we admire it. The other is quiet and gets respect. What I tell you will give you a start on respect.

We've been struggling with type for over five centuries. There aren't many surprises left. But you need to pay a lot of attention to detail. You ought to learn about the things that make respected professionals look like ninnies and how to make sure they don't happen to you. To begin with, I'll give you three warnings. Let's look at them before we move on to typographic perils.

One. Don't trust a built-in hyphenation dictionary. Not many are any good, especially not on small computers. You have to check every word break yourself. And remember that three lines in a row, each with a break, is more than you'll normally get away with.

The gaps between sentences on the left are too wide.

The right column has one word-space between sentences. It has none in front of the W, which is a bit tight. It has half a space (half the point size) in front of the A.

O woman! Lovely woman. Nature made thee to temper man. We had been brutes without you. Angels are painted fair, to look like you.

O woman! Lovely woman. Nature made thee to temper man.We had been brutes without you.Angels are painted fair, to look like you.

Two. Don't trust programs that check spelling. They're good at some things but not everything. The spelling errors they leave behind make the author sound unhinged.

Three. Don't trust your typist. Beware of two wordspaces after a period, and paragraphs with three-inch indents. Good, professional typists are too often full of the rot they learned in typing classes.

Line length

Choose your line length (or column measure, if you like) carefully. If you change it later, you may have to redo other things, such as the hyphenation.

Most people are used to reading newspaper columns of about forty characters. They tend to have trouble with more than sixty characters to a line. Remember that Gutenberg's masterpiece, the forty-two line bible, had two-column pages.

Don't indent the first paragraph

An indent tells you that you've come to a paragraph break. Therefore, neither the first paragraph needs an indent, nor does the first after a subheading. In general, you need to mark the beginning of a new paragraph because the last line before a break might run the full width of the column.

Don't use capitals in body text, unless you HAVE to.

This rule has often been set aside, in newspaper work especially. News stories do change at the last moment before press time and that's not the best time to rearrange a paragraph for the sake of typographic excellence. You have a computer to work out the details, so there is no excuse for an indent in the first paragraph.

This DODIPOULE, this DIDOPPER, this professed poetical BRAGGART has railed upon me, without WIT or ART!

This *dodipoule*, this *didopper*, this professed poetical *braggart* has railed upon me, without *wit* or *art!*

Italics rather than caps

Capitals in any quantity disturb the texture of the column. Don't say THE EXECUTIVE COMMITTEE. Use italics instead. If your italics are much denser than the roman, and you want to avoid a dark patch in the column, you can try spacing them apart very slightly.

Linespace

The distance between lines is called leading. Printers used to add space between lines with strips of lead. Linespace is measured from baseline to baseline and this causes problems. What we see is far more important than what we measure, and what we see is the strip of white space between the lines. Here's an example.

Take out a few business cards and look at them. They usually have separate lines for the street, the city and the telephone number. The line with the phone number usually looks too close to the line above it. This is because numerals are higher than lower case letters and take up more of the white space between the lines. A line with a lot of numerals, or capitals, often needs extra leading.

The text on the left has 18.5 point leading. The second and the third line look too close together.

In the middle, the third line is leaded 20 points, the rest 17.75 points. That's about right.

On the right, the third line is leaded 21 points, the rest 17.25 points; a bit too much.

Wrathful
gypsy,
full of
curses

Wrathful
gypsy,
full of
curses

Wrathful
gypsy,
full of
curses

Lift the baseline

Parentheses are designed to fit the lower case letters. Next to capitals, they usually look too low: (Tt). Let's try moving the left parenthesis by shifting the baseline a touch. Many other bits of punctuation also look too low with caps. The hyphen is one: a-z looks all right, A-Z doesn't.

Add ligatures

In the old days, ligatures were a necessity. Metal type looked terrible without them. The text had light patches, because some fill   fill
fling   fling

The words on the left haven't got ligatures. Some typefaces suffer more than others when the letter f overlaps the dot of an i.

letter combinations didn't fit snugly together. The worst involved the f. Ligatures, character combinations on one piece of type, were used to avoid this problem. They aren't absolutely essential anymore, but certainly add a touch of grace. Most typefaces have the f-i and the f-l. Run 'search and replace' to exchange fi and fl for the ligatures fi and fl.

And finally...

Look through a few books. Joseph Blumenthal's *The Art of the Printed Book 1455 to 1955* is not a bad place to start. Neither is *The Typographic Book* by Stanley Morison and Kenneth Day. You can get them on inter-library loan. Select pages that you admire. Recreate them as accurately as your equipment will allow: you can learn a lot by imitation. Close scrutiny is the best way I know to acquire a trained eye.

Learn the rules and follow them the best you can. Not many people do. You'll be one of the masters.

References

Blumenthal, J. (1973). *The Art of the Printed Book 1455 to 1955.* The Pierpoint Morgan Library, New York; David R Godine, Boston.

Morison, S. and Day. (1963). *The Typographic Book 1450 to 1935.* Ernest Benn.

JAMES HARTLEY
The layout of computer-based text

INTRODUCTION

As I start to write this chapter I have in front of me the draft of a questionnaire on management training. The text is clearly computer-based and to my mind full of problems. First of all, the top and the bottom of the information area are heavily ruled, creating a rigid framework. Then each item of the questionnaire is placed in a separate box. The width of each box is pre-determined, in order to form a two-column layout, but the depth varies according to the amount of information per item. The information is forced to fit in this width and this is sometimes achieved by using different typesizes. Finally, there are instructional notes, commentaries and directions, also boxed and printed in a larger typesize on a grey tinted background. Figure 1 provides an illustration.

Now it may be that text like this presents no problems to people familiar with computer-based text. But to me, brought up in a world of manual typewriters and hot-metal printing, I find the presentation of this questionnaire to be mildly distasteful. So the purpose of this chapter is to describe some basic notions about typographic layout and to discuss how they might apply to both screen-based and computer-based printed text.

I hope to achieve this in a relatively informal manner and without making references to supporting documentation, but I shall conclude the chapter with a brief bibliography of related research for those who are interested in reading more.

In this chapter I shall discuss two main issues, namely:
(1) relationships between space and structure in text; and
(2) issues concerning access and emphasis in text.
But before I do this I need to make one more point. The

Figure 1. A page from a draft of an unpublished questionnaire

DRAFT

1.4 *How long did the activity last?*

• *For a stand-alone event (e.g., a training course or study visit), please give the number of days involved.*

• *For an intermittent or periodic activity (e.g., receiving guidance from a mentor, or on-the-job training), please give an approximate number of equivalent days for the whole year. (Cumulative 8 hours = 1 day)*

Number of days ☐

1.5 *How much non-work time did participation in this event or activity require? (e.g., home study, or attendance out of normal working hours.)*

No non-work time was involved ☐

Number of hours of non-work time ☐

1.6 *What was the main topic?*

[ ]

1.7 *Was this activity related to your professional, technical or functional development, or to your development as a manager?*

Solely professional, technical or functional ☐

Mainly professional, technical or functional ☐

About half professional/technical/ functional and about half management ☐

Mainly management ☐

Solely management ☐

1.8 *Was this event or activity*

Your idea? ☐

An idea jointly from you and your organisation? ☐

Your organisation's idea? ☐

Other *(please specify)* [ ]

1.9 *How do you rate the value of this event or activity* **for your present job?**

Very little help ☐

Little help ☐

Some help ☐

Very helpful ☐

Very great help ☐

1.10 *How do you rate the likely value of this event or activity* **for your future career?**

Likely to be of very little help ☐

Likely to be of little help ☐

Likely to be of some help ☐

Likely to be very helpful ☐

Likely to be of very great help ☐

Don't know ☐

1.11 *To what extent has your organisation encouraged you to make use of this training in your job?*

No encouragement at all ☐

Some limited encouragement ☐

Much encouragement ☐

A great deal of encouragement ☐

Not applicable ☐

PLEASE MOVE DIRECTLY TO SECTION 3 ON PAGE 7

1.6 Was this event or activity related to your **general management** development, or to **some other specialist professional, technical or functional** development?

Solely professional, technical or functional ☐

Mainly professional, technical or functional ☐

About half professional/technical/ functional and about half management ☐

Mainly management ☐

Solely management ☐

1.7 Was this event or activity

Your idea? ☐

An idea jointly from you and your organisation? ☐

Your organisation's idea? ☐

Other *(please specify)*

1.8 Who paid for it?

I paid for it myself ☐

I paid most, but my organisation contributed ☐

My organisation paid most, but I contributed ☐

My organisation paid for it, or provided it ☐

My organisation paid, but I must repay the cost if I leave within a specified time ☐

It was covered by a government/ local authority/T.E.C. grant ☐

It was free ☐

Other *(please specify)*

1.9 How do you rate the value of this event or activity **for your present job?**

Very little help ☐

Little help ☐

Some help ☐

Very helpful ☐

Very great help ☐

1.10 How do you rate the likely value of this event or activity **for your future career?**

Likely to be of very little help ☐

Likely to be of little help ☐

Likely to be of some help ☐

Likely to be very helpful ☐

Likely to be of very great help ☐

Don't know ☐

1.11 To what extent has your organisation encouraged you to make use of this training in your job?

Not applicable ☐

No encouragement at all ☐

Some limited encouragement ☐

Much encouragement ☐

A great deal of encouragement ☐

PLEASE MOVE DIRECTLY TO SECTION 3 ON PAGE 7

Figure 2. A revised
version of Figure 1

questionnaire referred to was a draft, both in terms of its layout
and its content. Figure 2 shows the final version of the same page.
Here the presentation is clearly tidier. One of the advantages of
desktop publishing is that one can explore possibilities. But what
should guide this exploration, especially when the setting of the
text is complex?

SPACE AND STRUCTURE

It is surprising to me how, in many discussions about typography,
interest centres on typefaces and typesizes. To my mind, as shown
in Figures 1 and 2, what is more important is the interrelationship
between the 'white space' and the text. Basically, what determines
the line lengths and the chosen typesizes is the overall size and
orientation of the page itself, and how one organises the white
space within this framework is crucial to making the text legible.
This argument applies to text on screens as well as to text on
paper. Typically, screens of today are set 'landscape' as opposed to
'portrait' (i.e. they are wider than they are tall) and, furthermore,
they (typically) contain only about 20 lines of text, thus making the
screen page much smaller than say an A5 or A4 printed page.
These limitations, however, are probably only temporary ones.
Much larger 'portrait' screen sizes will soon be widely available
which will present the equivalent of single or double A4 page
spreads. Whatever the size of the page or the screen, however, my
argument is the same: the overall size and orientation of the page
or screen determines what can be presented to the reader, and how
one organises the space in this framework is important. Space can
be systematically organised to show the structure of the text.

Horizontal spacing

Figure 3 illustrates this argument in a general sense. In Figure 3a
the text is set 'justified': this means that there is a straight right-
hand edge as well as a straight left-hand one. Straight right-hand
edges are achieved by varying the interword spacing and by using
(occasionally) hyphenation. The use of such justified text is
widespread in page layouts but it is not so common in (small)
screen-based texts. Here the preference seems to be more for the
style of layout shown in Figure 3b.

Figure 3b shows the same text as that shown in Figure 3a, but

Figure 3a

Figure 3b

Now the sons of Jacob were twelve. The sons of Leah; Reuben, Jacob's firstborn, and Simeon, and Levi, and Judah, and Issachar, and Zebulun. The sons of Rachel; Joseph, and Benjamin: And the sons of Bilhah, Rachel's handmaid; Dan, and Naphtali. And the sons of Zilpah, Leah's handmaid; Gad, and Asher. These are the sons of Jacob, which were born to him in Padan-aram.

Now the sons of Jacob were twelve. The sons of Leah; Reuben, Jacob's firstborn, and Simeon, and Levi, and Judah, and Issachar, and Zebulun. The sons of Rachel; Joseph, and Benjamin: And the sons of Bilhah, Rachel's handmaid; Dan, and Naphtali. And the sons of Zilpah, Leah's handmaid; Gad and Asher. These are the sons of Jacob, which were born to him in Padan-aram.

now the text is set 'unjustified': this means that there is now a ragged right-hand margin (as in normal typescript). In Figure 3b the spacing between the words is regular and consistent.

Figure 3. Six versions of the same text to show how spacing can clarify text structure

Many investigators in the field of printed text have made direct experimental comparisons between justified and unjustified text. The majority of these studies have found no significant differences on search and retrieval tasks and on tests of reading speed and reading comprehension, although there is some suggestion that unjustified text is more suitable for younger children and older adults. Furthermore, the actual line length of the text is an important consideration and so too is the difficulty of the text. Shorter line lengths do not lend themselves so well to justified text, and multisyllabic text is difficult to read when set unjustified on short lines.

However, the debate about justified versus unjustified text can get more complex. With justified text the print is forced to fit the column width by default. With unjustified text there is no need to fill the line with text just because the space is there. This means, for example, that one can consider other rules for determining the line endings (and even the beginnings) of individual lines. Figures 3c, 3d, 3e and 3f illustrate these points.

In Figure 3c, for instance, the line endings are determined by syntactic considerations: here each line ends at a syntactic point. Figure 3d takes the argument further. Here the beginning and the ending of each line is determined by the sense of the text and syntactic groupings rather than in an arbitrary manner (as in Figure 3a). In Figure 3e the grouping of the parts of the text is made

Figure 3c

Now the sons of Jacob were twelve:
The sons of Leah;
Reuben, Jacob's firstborn,
and Simeon, and Levi, and Judah,
and Issachar, and Zebulun:
The sons of Rachel;
Joseph, and Benjamin:
And the sons of Bilhah, Rachel's handmaid;
Dan, and Naphtali:
And the sons of Zilpah, Leah's handmaid;
Gad, and Asher:
These are the sons of Jacob, which were born
to him in Padan-aram.

Figure 3d

Now the sons of Jacob were twelve:
The sons of Leah;
    Reuben, Jacob's firstborn,
    and Simeon, and Levi, and Judah,
    and Issachar, and Zebulun:
The sons of Rachel;
    Joseph, and Benjamin:
And the sons of Bilhar, Rachel's handmaid;
    Dan, and Naphtali:
And the sons of Zilpah, Leah's handmaid;
    Gad, and Asher:
These are the sons of Jacob, which were born
to him in Padan-aram.

Figure 3e

Now the sons of Jacob were twelve:
    The sons of Leah;
        Reuben, Jacob's firstborn,
        and Simeon, and Levi, and Judah,
        and Issachar, and Zebulun:
    The sons of Rachel;
        Joseph, and Benjamin:
    And the sons of Bilhar, Rachel's handmaid;
        Dan, and Naphtali:
    And the sons of Zilpah, Leah's handmaid;
        Gad, and Asher:
These are the sons of Jacob, which were born
to him in Padan-aram.

Figure 3f

Now the sons of Jacob were twelve:

    The sons of Leah;
        Reuben, Jacob's firstborn,
        and Simeon, and Levi, and Judah,
        and Issachar, and Zebulun:

    The sons of Rachel;
        Joseph, and Benjamin:

    And the sons of Bilhar, Rachel's handmaid;
        Dan, and Naphtali:

    And the sons of Zilpah, Leah's handmaid;
        Gad, and Asher:

These are the sons of Jacob, which were born
to him in Padan-aram.

clearer by using space to show an 'introduction' and a 'conclusion', and in Figure 3f this is amplified further by the use of additional interline space to group and separate the parts.

Much research has been devoted to examining the merits of 'chunking' printed text in this way. Computer programmes have been written which produce text with line endings determined by text difficulty or syntactic considerations. Parallel studies have been made of various ways to chunk electronic text. Such studies have pointed to possible advantages and disadvantages of the approach.

I have, of course, especially chosen the text shown in Figure 3 to make my points about the interrelationship of space and structure. Although this particular text exaggerates the case, I shall use it to make three more points. These are that:

1) Research (with much less poetic text) has shown that readers prefer lists of points or items to be set out vertically (and possibly indented) rather than run on in continuous text.

2) Opening up the spatial components of text makes the text easier to to read and easier to learn. Veronica Casey, one of my undergraduates, recently showed in an experimental study that eleven-year-old children recalled 20% more of text set in the format shown in Figure 3d than that shown in Figure 3a.

3) The format of the text affects the way it is recalled. Ninety-five per cent of undergraduates, presented with either Figure 3a or 3d, will write it out in the same format in an immediate recall test. Similar results have been found with 12-13 year-old children. Thus the layout of text can help the ways in which people both learn and remember.

Vertical spacing

So far in this discussion I have concentrated on the horizontal spacing of the text. I now want to turn to the vertical spacing. Essentially my argument is very similar to that outlined above: one can use consistent amounts of vertical space between elements in the text down the page

Essentially my argument is very similar to that outlined above: one can use consistent amounts of vertical space between elements in the text down the page which will help the reader to perceive the text's underlying structure.

Main heading

Units of line feed can be used consistently to separate out components of the text – such as sentences, paragraphs, secondary and tertiary headings.

Secondary heading

One simple way of using line-feed to do this is to use a proportional spacing system.
One can, for example, with complex text, start each new sentence on a new line (i.e. no extra line feed).
One can then separate paragraphs by a line space – as in this example (i.e. one extra line feed).

One can then separate secondary headings from the paragraphs by providing two extra line spaces above and one below; and one can separate main headings from the text by providing four extra line spaces above and two below.
(Perhaps I should comment, again, that students rate complex text spaced out in this manner as easier to read than text set more traditionally.)

If you then feel that the amount of vertical space is excessive, then the scheme can be modified, as in this example. Here I have used two lines of space above and one below a primary heading, and one line of space above and none below a secondary one, but I have added in typographic cues (capital letters and italics) to enhance this spatial arrangement.

MAIN HEADING

Units of line feed can be used consistently to separate out components of the text – such as sentences, paragraphs, secondary and tertiary headings.

Secondary heading
One simple way of using line-feed to do this is to use a proportional spacing system.
One can, for example, with complex text, start each new sentence on a new line (i.e. no extra line feed).
One can then separate paragraphs by a line space - as in this example (i.e. one extra line feed).

One can then separate secondary headings from the paragraphs by providing one line space above; and one can separate main headings from the text by providing two extra line spaces above and one below.
(Perhaps I should comment, again, that students rate complex text spaced out in this manner as easier to read than text set more traditionally.)

Figure 4. Two examples of consistent vertical spacing

to help the reader perceive the text's underlying structure. Units of line feed can be used consistently to separate out components of the text - such as sentences, paragraphs, secondary and tertiary headings. Figure 4 shows two examples.

In typical printed text, of course, the vertical spacing is not consistent. The vertical space is pushed and pulled about in order to make the text fit into the space available, and to have a fixed baseline which is the same on every page. Under my system the baseline is not fixed: the text stops at a meaningful point. I suggest that a useful rule is to have a notional fixed depth (say a specified number of lines) plus or minus two. In short, I argue for the same flexibility in vertical text as I do for horizontal text, and I would not expect the text to stop at the same point on every page. (I will be interested to see what the designers of this text do in this respect!)

Spacing around other elements

This argument can be extended to the presentation of other elements in the text. Thus, for example, one can consistently use one unit of space above a table caption, or the start of a figure, when these elements are embedded in the text. Similarly, one can use one unit of line space below the bottom line or rule of a table, or below a figure caption.

Space and tabular layouts

Indeed, one can even extend the argument to the layout of tables themselves. A considerable body of evidence shows that tables are easier to read and understand if space is used consistently to show their underlying structure. One rule of thumb is that if a table contains several rows of items then it is appropriate to group the rows by leaving a line space, say, between every five entries. Furthermore, the space between the columns also needs to be appropriate so that the right data are grouped together. Thus there is no need to balance tables in the centre or across a page and to vary the internal spacing just to make them fit. A common error is shown in Figure 5. Here in Table 1, there are four columns of print: and in Table 2 there are six. The printer, however, has varied the internal spacing to make both tables fit the same width.

Table 1

Table 2

A	B	C	D
11	22	33	44
22	33	44	55
33	44	55	66
44	55	66	77
55	66	77	88

A	B	C	D	E	F
11	22	33	44	55	66
22	33	44	55	66	77
33	44	55	66	77	88
44	55	66	77	88	99
55	66	77	88	99	11

Figure 5. Table 1 contains 4 columns: Table 2 contains 6 columns. Although the information is the same for Columns A, B, C & D, the spatial arrangement has been altered in Table 2 to make the table have the same width as Table 1. In my view Table 2 should be set with the same inter-column spacing as Table 1, or vice versa

My argument is that this is inappropriate: tables 1 and 2 should be set with the same inter-column spacing. Tables can be set unjustified too!

Finally, may I note in this respect that if several tables of the same kind are to be presented, then it should go without saying that it is appropriate to keep them in the same format throughout the text. However, this does not always happen. In an article I was reading recently, for example, the first four tables were in the format:

	1	2
A	–	–
B	–	–

but the last one, for some reason, was presented:

	A	B
1	–	–
2	–	–

and this lead me to misread it.

Positioning tables in the text

The positioning of tables in the text (and other illustrative matter, too) also deserves more consideration than it usually gets. In scientific articles, for example, it is not unusual to find tables divorced from their textual reference because of the standard practice of positioning such materials at the top or bottom of a column of print. In the journals that I typically read, such mismatches occur about 25% of the time. The most common fault in the *Journal of Educational Psychology*, for example, is for the author to describe the last table of results in the 'Results' section but for this table to be printed in the following 'Discussion' section. Clearly it is not always possible to print tables in their appropriate sections, especially when there are runs of several tables, large tables, and page turn-over decisions to be made. However, one currently gets the impression that designers do not always consider the reader when they position tables in what, for them, are convenient places.

Planning spacing and the grid

The point I need to make most forcefully here is that, in order to achieve consistency in spacing of the kind outlined in the sections above, one has to plan in advance. Decisions about spacing have to be made and adhered to throughout the presentation of the text.

One aid in this respect is the typographic reference grid. Grids help designers to be consistent in their use of horizontal and vertical spacing throughout the text and to achieve the necessary balance between consistency and flexibility. In terms of this text chapter for instance, one could use the same underlying grid for each double-page spread by providing a grid with horizontal lines, one for each possible line of text, and vertical lines to represent the position of the margins. The same units of line feed would then be used systematically throughout the text to indicate the spacing of the sections, the paragraphs, the illustrative inserts and their captions.

In the olden days galley proofs of the text would be pasted on to these grids to the designer's specification. Today electronic templates are being developed that fulfil this purpose although, even here, the authors of electronic texts sometimes first prepare their text on specially prepared grids that match the screen format. As with printed text, each grid specifies the number of lines and the number and position of the characters available on each line for one screen page. In addition, space is provided at the side of each grid for recording the more technical requirements, such as whether a word is to be presented in a different colour or flashed in reverse video.

Finally in this section I should note the somewhat obvious fact that much of what I have had to say about the vertical spacing of text is difficult to achieve on a small screen. Here designers find themselves forced to use different features to emphasise structure, and it is to features such as these that the discussion now turns.

ACCESS AND EMPHASIS IN TEXT

Access

Readers rarely read texts from start to finish, and they need to be able to locate different sets of information quickly. Authors, printers and designers utilize a number of different devices to help readers gain access to the text and to find their way around it. Typical examples include contents pages, indexes, abstracts/summaries, running heads, headings in the text, numbered sections and/or paragraphs, and the page numbers themselves. All of these devices need careful thought in their design, especially when presented on the small screen. Again, my argument is for consistency of presentation and for careful attention to be paid to the 'white space' that surrounds these 'access structures'.

Emphasis in text

Typographic cues are commonly used in print to emphasize different points within the text, as well as to help indicate its overall arrangement. Typographers can convey emphasis by using capital letters, emboldened print, italic typefaces, boxes, underlining and colour. Such devices can draw the reader's attention to a particular word or point, or help the reader to discern the overall structure of the text. In this chapter the designers have used typographic cues with the headings to enhance the spatial arrangement.

Combining cues

Most of the access and typographic cues listed above have been subjected to research on their effectiveness. However, most of this research has considered a particular cue or feature in isolation (for example, there are studies of text with and without headings) whereas most text, of course, combines the use of cues. When considering the effectiveness of multiple cueing, a distinction has to be drawn, I think, between using different cues for different purposes (e.g. the use of bold type to indicate that a word is explained in a glossary and italic to indicate emphasis) and multiple cueing for a single purpose (e.g. the use of both bold type and italic to emphasise a word). I am suggesting in the latter case that really there is no need to use several cues when one will do. It hardly seems necessary, in my view, to emphasize a heading by printing it in a different format (say capitals), different typeface (say sans serif), a different size (say 14 point) and a different colour (say red). One of these cues is probably sufficient.

The use of colour

In my view additional colour should be used sparingly in printed
or electronic text. It seems to me that colour has two overlapping
functions: (1) it can make the presentation of the text look more
attractive (if it is not overdone), and (2) it can clarify the structure
of the text. Coloured pictures, added to embellish a printed text,
illustrate this first purpose. Colour added to explicate a diagram
illustrates the second one. Headings, set in a different colour from
the body of text, illustrate the overlap between these two
functions.

Clearly one of the most important features of electronic text is
the availability of multi-coloured formats. In some systems many
colours are used, but with Ceefax, Oracle and Prestel, seven
colours are used (although each can form the background for the
others). These seven are green, red, blue, magenta, cyan, yellow
and white.

Colour cueing can be used in electronic text in the same way
that italic or bold print can be used in printed text to emphasize a
particular word or phrase: for example, one might use red for 'do
not ...'. Colour can be also used in electronic text to indicate
categories of importance – such as in the News on Ceefax, where
the main paragraphs appear in white and the subparagraphs in blue.
Colour can also be used in place of space to convey organization
and structure. Thus rows or columns in tables (or groups of them)
may be presented in alternating colours to aid retrieval. Studies
show, however, that this can cause the readers difficulties if they
are expected to read both down and across the tables.

One particular problem with using colour cueing in text is that,
unlike spatial cueing, there does not appear to be an intuitive range
of colours that suggests a hierarchy of importance. In addition, if
colours are to be used in a meaningful way, then users must be able
to distinguish between the functions of different colours, and thus
the colour coding must not be excessive. The number of colours
used on any one graph or chart must be kept to a minimum, they
should be used consistently, and they need to be clearly
differentiated from other colours used elsewhere, such as in the
wording of items on the screen.

Colour on colour

An additional but related problem is that it is, of course, possible to use different coloured backgrounds for electronic text (in much the same way as one can use different coloured paper in conventional printing). However, when two colours are presented in close juxtaposition then the perception of each colour is modified by the other. Thus the perception of sizes indicated by bar charts, for example, may depend upon the foreground and surrounding colours: warm colours (red and yellow), for instance, usually appear larger than cool colours (green and blue). Also, when selecting colour on colour combinations, dark colours (red and blue) should be paired with light ones (white, yellow, cyan) and two light or two medium colours (green and magenta) should not be used together. Clearly there is a great deal more research to be done here on people's preferences for colour combinations and on how to use colour both sparingly and consistently.

A FINAL WORD . . .

It will come as no surprise to the reader to find that in concluding this chapter I want 1) to re-emphasise simplicity and clarity in the layout of printed and electronic text, and 2) to reiterate the importance of planned spacing.

Let me conclude with a final example. In a study I carried out some years ago I asked a number of research workers to indicate their preferences for the design and layout of the references which occur at the end of a scientific article. Essentially there were four basic comparisons, with a number of variants in each. The four basic layouts to be compared were:

1. Conventional arrangement without typographic cues

2. Conventional arrangement with typographic cues

3. Spaced arrangement without typographic cues

4. Spaced arrangement with typographic cues

Figure 6 shows just one individual reference set in these four modes. The judges had to compare lists of references set in these

1. Huchingson, R.D., Williams, R.D., Reid, T.G. & Dudek, C.L. (1981). Formatting, message load, sequencing method and presentation rate for computer-generated displays. Human Factors, 23, 5, 551-559.

2. Huchingson, R.D., Williams, R.D., Reid, T.G. & Dudek, C.L. (1981). Formatting, message load, sequencing method and presentation rate for computer-generated displays. *Human Factors*, 23, 5, 551-559.

3. Huchingson, R.D., Williams, R.D., Reid, T.G. & Dudek, C.L. (1981).
   Formatting, message load, sequency method and presentation rate for computer-generated displays.
   Human Factors, 23, 5, 551-559.

4. Huchingson, R.D., Williams, R.D., Reid, T.G. & Dudek, C.L. (1981).
   Formatting, message load, sequency method and presentation rate for computer-generated displays.
   Human Factors, 23, 5, 551-559.

Figure 6. Four layouts of the same reference designed to illustrate how spacing is more important than typographic cueing in depicting structure

modes and, using the method of paired comparisons, to determine which one they preferred most, which one next, etc.

The results were clear cut: the judges preferred the spatial arrangements to the conventional ones, and they preferred versions with typographic cues to versions without them. This meant that version 4 was preferred most, and that version 3 was next. Version 2 came next and version 1 was preferred least. In line with the argument presented in this chapter I want to emphasize that the spatial arrangements without typographic cues were preferred to the conventional arrangements with them.

Acknowledgements

I am grateful to Mrs Margaret Woodward and Mrs Jenny Everill for assistance with the preparation of this chapter, and to the original producers of Figures 1 and 2 who kindly allowed me to reproduce them.

Suggested further reading

BLACK, A. (1990). *Typefaces for Desktop Publishing: A User Guide.*
London: Architecture Design and Technology Press.
A more thoughtful book than most in this field.

DUMAS, J.S. (1988). *Designing User Interfaces for Software.* Englewood
Cliffs, N.J.: Prentice Hall.
Useful, readable paperback on the issues discussed in this chapter, and
more.

HARTLEY, J. (1985). *Designing Instructional Text* (2nd edition). London:
Kogan Page.
Basic text on the design of printed text, with one chapter on electronic
text.

HARTLEY, J. (Ed.) (1992). *Technology and Writing.* London: Jessica
Kingsley.
Contains chapters on writing for electronic text, and one on screen
density.

HELANDER, M. (Ed.) (1988). *Handbook of Human-Computer Interaction.*
Amsterdam: Elevier Science Publishers B.V. (North Holland).
A compendium of useful chapters on electronic text, heavily research
based, and including ones on the design of menus, screens, windows and
text.

MILES, J. (1987). *Design for Desktop Publishing.* London: Gordon Fraser.
General guidelines illustrating what can be achieved with desktop
publishing.

RIVLIN, C., LEWIS, R., AND COOPER, R.D. (Eds.) (1990).
Guidelines for Screen Design. Oxford: Blackwell Scientific Publications.
Useful general discussion of screen design. Includes colour illustrations.

RICHARD SOUTHALL

Presentation rules and rules of composition

Presentation rules and generalized markup

The orthodoxy of generalized markup sees a document as an assembly of *content objects* of different types.[1] These objects, which are defined in a *document type definition* appropriate for the document in question, are identified and delimited in the machine-readable *virtual document* which is the document's primary mode of existence. If a human reader needs to be given access to the document's content, an *actual document* is produced.

Actual documents consist of arrays of marks on a display surface. In documents written with alphabetic or syllabic scripts, the marks are *character images*. These are grouped into *word images*, which are arranged horizontally on the display surface to form *word image rows*. A vertical succession of word image rows forms a rectangular or quasi-rectangular *word image block*, and it is these blocks which realize the content objects of the document.

If an actual document is to be produced from the marked-up virtual document, a set of *presentation rules* is associated with each type of content object in the document. These rules govern the metric properties of the word image block by which the object is realized in the actual document and its metric relationships with adjacent blocks. The notion is that different sets of rules can be associated with the same virtual document to produce actual documents whose appearances differ but whose meaning is the same.

The content of presentation rules

Presentation rules, like content objects in generalized markup, are

[1] This paper uses the terminology for documents and their components proposed in [Southall88].

arranged hierarchically. At the top of the hierarchy are rules which dictate the maximum width and depth of the word image blocks in a document, their locations relative to the edges of the display surface, and the sets of fonts from which the character images in them are derived. Further down, rules for the presentation of the blocks which realize each type of content object dictate the separation between successive word image rows in the block (*line spacing* or *leading*); the ways in which the ends of the rows are aligned with one another (*alignment* or *justification*); their horizontal positions relative to the ends of rows of the maximum width permitted in the document (*indents*); and the vertical separation between the block and the blocks which precede and follow it (*spacing before* and *spacing after*). They may also dictate, for documents printed on paper, whether or not the block may be divided across a page break (*keep together*), whether a page break is permissible after the block (*keep with next*), and whether the block should start a fresh page (*page break before*).[2]

Rules of composition
Metric relationships in the word image row
The metric properties of a word image block, and the metric relationships between the word image rows of which it is made up, are not enough on their own to provide a complete description of the block's configuration. The metric relationships within rows – between the character images within word images, and between the word images in a row – also have to be taken into account.

The specifications for the metric relationships between the character images in a word image come from the font from which the character images are derived. The font contains, or has associated with it, a *width table* which specifies the set-width of each character, and a *kerning table* which specifies modifications to characters' set-widths according to the identity of the character which follows them in the word image. Thus specifying the font from which word images are derived is normally sufficient to specify the metric relationships within them.

The metric relationships between the word images in a word

---

[2]All these rules, and most of the names for them, are taken from the Format Paragraph menu in Microsoft Word for Windows version 1.1.

image row, however, are not always determined exclusively by information which comes from the font metrics. In unjustified (ragged-right, ragged-left or centred) setting, the spaces between word images in successive rows have a constant value. This is normally the width of the space character in the font, which is specified in the font metrics. In justified setting, on the other hand, where the right-hand ends of the rightmost word images in successive rows are aligned vertically on the display surface, the interword spaces in general vary from row to row. The range of values assigned to interword spaces in justified setting, and the actions to be taken when the value of the interword space required to justify a row falls outside this range, are indeed specified by rules: but these rules; although they make use of information which comes from the font metrics, are characteristics of the document formatting system itself.[3]

It follows from this that presentation rules which specify the metric properties and relationships of word image blocks, and the fonts to be used in them, do not suffice to specify completely the configuration of an actual document. The rules which govern the behaviour of the system with which the document is formatted also play their part in deciding its configuration. In a document containing justified word image blocks, the rules in question are those which specify the maximum and minimum values of interword space and the rules for dividing words. Even if all the word image blocks in the document are unjustified, the formatting system may still have a part to play: its rules for word division may be invoked, for example, if the specification for the word image blocks calls for differences in the lengths of adjacent word image rows to be maintained at less than a certain level (cf. [Mittelbach & Rowley92]).

The rules which a formatting system uses to assign values to interword spaces in justified text, and to decide on the locations at which words are divided, are examples of the system's *rules of composition*.

---

[3]Knuth's TEX is exceptional among document formatting systems in that the maximum amounts by which interword spaces are allowed to stretch and shrink in justified setting, as well as a value for their normal width, are specified in the metrics of all the fonts the system uses.

Spacing rules and rules of orthography
The rules of composition which are invoked in the formatting of justified text are of two kinds. They deal on the one hand with the values of interword spaces, and on the other with the division of words.[4] The difference between them illustrates a more general separation of rules of composition into two classes. One class deals with the allocation of white space in the line of text, and the other with the sequence of characters and spaces of which the line itself is made up. We may call these two classes of rules of composition *spacing rules* and *rules of orthography* respectively.

Compositional environments
Lamport's LaTeX document formatting system, following Reid's SCRIBE, has the concept of an *environment* [Lamport86, p. 34]. This is a delimited component of a document's text, within which particular sets of presentation rules apply to certain types of content objects in the text. Thus, for example, LaTeX has environments called *itemize* and *enumerate*, both of which may contain objects called *items*. In an actual document formatted with LaTeX, each of the word image blocks which realizes an item from an *itemize* environment is marked with a label, while those from an *enumerate* environment are numbered in ascending order. The label character and the numbering system used for enumeration are specified for each type of environment in the set of presentation rules which LaTeX calls the *document style*.

   In a similar way, we can think of a *compositional environment* as a component of the text of a document within which particular sets of rules of composition apply. Compositional environments may be large-scale objects in a text, such as passages of mathematical setting or tabular matter; or they may be much smaller-scale objects such as proper names or the titles of books or journals.

Formalizations of rules of composition in different types of system
Every kind of document formatting system has rules of composition because every system is faced with similar problems in composing text. What differs between one kind of system and another is the extent to which formal definitions of the rules are

---

[4]In systems which justify a slack line by adding space between characters, rules of the first kind deal with intercharacter as well as interword spaces (*cf.* [Seybold79, p 219]).

built into the structure of the system itself. At one extreme are computer-based systems for formatting generically marked-up text, in which every feature of an actual document which is not specified by a presentation rule or by the sequence of characters in the text itself must necessarily be determined by a formally defined rule of composition. At the other extreme is the hand compositor, whose freedom of action is limited only by the physical characteristics of the equipment of composition – the dimensions of the composing stick and of the types and spaces with which the text is composed. Between these extremes lie hot-metal type-composing and early photocomposing machines. In these systems, although the allocation of interword space values in a justified line is carried out mechanically, the operator has wide discretion in deciding on the sequence of characters in the line, the positioning of fixed spaces, the location of line-endings and the division of words.

Rules of composition in compositors' manuals

Until the last decade of the nineteenth century, the technique used to compose texts with metal type was essentially the same as that described by Joseph Moxon in his *Mechanick exercises* of 1683 [Moxon83, ch. 22].[5] Metal types are taken one at a time out of a type-case and arranged in a composing-stick (or *stick* for short). For each piece of text to be composed, the end-pieces of the stick are set to a fixed distance apart, called the *measure*.

The compositor chooses a type corresponding to each successive letter of each word of the text and puts it in the composing-stick. As each word is completed, a space is put in the line after it; and the process is continued until the line of types fills or almost fills the width of the stick, which is the measure.

The compositor normally has available three different widths of interword space for setting text. These are *thin, mid* and *thick spaces*, with widths respectively one-fifth, one-fourth and one-third of the body size of the type with which the line is set. The compositor also has *em quadrats* or *quads*, as wide as the body size, and *en quads*, half the width of the em quad. There are also very thin spaces, one or one-and-a-half points wide, called *hair spaces*.

---

[5]A more recent account, with clearer illustrations than Moxon's, is in [Simon68].

If the line of types in the stick reaches the end of a word and does not quite fill the measure, the compositor replaces the interword spaces with wider spaces until the measure is full; or, conversely, if the measure is filled and the last word in the line has one or two characters still unset, he replaces the interword spaces with narrower ones so as to get in the remaining characters. If the measure is filled at the middle of a word, the compositor chooses a suitable place to divide the word and adjusts the interword spaces in the line to accommodate the first part of the divided word and the hyphen that accompanies it.[6]

Interword spaces in justified text
Two criteria for well-composed text are unanimously stated in the compositors' manuals. One is that the interword spaces should be narrow in relation to the appearing size of the type; the other that they should be optically, rather than mechanically, equal.

> 'It is not difficult to define close spacing, and it is not difficult to achieve it . . . as far as possible the space between words should be approximately of the same width throughout, and that is the width of the letter i'[7] [Jennett64, p. 255].

> 'In book-work it is required that the space between the words of a line shall seem uniform in width, but to produce this appearance of uniformity spaces of different thickness must be selected for use between [characters] of unlike form' [DeVinne04, p. 88].

The appearing width of an interword space varies with the shapes of the characters on either side of it. Parallel vertical strokes facing one another on either side of a space, as in **d b**, make the space appear narrower than its actual width, while between round characters such as **e o**, or diagonals as in **y w**, it appears wider.

---

[6]It is clear from this description that the exact location of every linebreak in a hand-composed text was the result of a conscious decision by the compositor. This contrasts with the view implicitly taken by present-day document formatting systems, which is that linebreaks in justified text are adventitious and mechanical interruptions to an essentially continuous sequence of word images.

[7]*i.e.* about one-third of the em, or a thick space's width.

Uniformity of interword spacing from line to line is seen as very important.

'Not only should the spaces be optically equal in the line, they should be equal, or more or less so, over the whole book' [Jennett64, p. 51].

'A reader is repelled by print in which words have been separated, as they may be occasionally, by two three-to-em spaces in the first and by [single] five-to-em spaces in the next line. Spacing of either kind . . . is a disgrace to the printer; it is a fault for which there is seldom acceptable excuse' [De Vinne01, p. 198].

Adding and removing space

When a line is almost full, or just overfull, the compositor often has to add or remove amounts of space which are too small to distribute over all the interword spaces in the line. This can be done without disturbing the apparent uniformity of the spacing, if the points at which spaces are changed are carefully chosen:

> '. . . if only a single space needs to be changed to justify the line, a wider space should be placed after punctuation marks, beginning with the full point; or, if there is no punctuation in the line, at the clearest break in the sense[8] . . .' [Brun25, p. 49].

> 'When one or two letters require to be got in, or to be driven out, the difference between a thick space and a middling one [*i.e.* between the normal interword space and the next narrower one] is not perceptible to the eye, particularly if the compositor is careful to place the latter before or after a v or w, after a comma that comes before a v or w, or after a y . . .' [Savage41, p. 179].

Spaces after full points

The rules for spacing after full points[9] are a subset of a much larger set of rules dealing with the spaces around punctuation marks.

---

[8] *á une espèce de césure la plus sensible*.

[9] *Full point* is printers' English for full stop. *Period* is the American equivalent, in both printers' and normal usage. Similarly, the English *exclamation mark* is the American *exclamation point*.

Unlike the rules for interword spacing in text, some of these rules vary considerably between one graphic culture and another. This is strikingly illustrated by the transatlantic differences in the rules for spacing after full points at the ends of sentences:

'The space after a full point should normally be the regular word space of the line. Em spaces, last remnant of the degenerate typography of the nineteenth century, break up the appearance of the page and should not be tolerated' [Tschichold67, p. 36; written in Switzerland in 1935].

'[There is] a modern tendency to use only the same amount of space following a period as between words in the same line; but in the [United States] Government Printing Office the em quad is used' [USGPO62].

The rules which govern the spacing around a punctuation mark do not depend simply on the identity of the character realized by the mark, but also on the semantic role the character plays in the text. Thus a full point denoting abbreviation is spaced differently from a full point marking the end of a sentence:

'The space after a comma or an abbreviating period may be thinner than that used after an unpointed word. These may seem trifling niceties, but their neglect damages the appearance of print' [DeVinne04, p. 88].

Here the purpose of the rule is to ensure that the appearing spaces after commas, abbreviations and unabbreviated words within a sentence are all equal, so that they are not confused with the wider space at the end of the sentence. The white space above a comma or a full point adds to the appearing width of the interword space which follows it, and the actual width of the space has to be decreased in consequence.

The rules for spacing around punctuation marks, like other spacing rules, refer to the visual rather than the graphic structure of the document. The content of a rule is modified according to the visual context of the marks to which it applies:

'Another rule that is inculcated into beginners, is, to use an m-quadrat after a full-point; but at the same time they should be informed, not to do it, where an Author is too sententious, and makes several short periods [*i.e.* sentences] in one paragraph. In such case the many blanks of m-quadrats will be contemptuously called *Pigeon-Holes* . . .' [Smith55, p. 113].

'When the words of a line have to be thin-spaced, the em quadrat that divides sentences in that line should be replaced by an en quadrat or a three-to-em space' [DeVinne04, p. 89].

Ending the line
Lines of type justified to a fixed measure, and with acceptable interword spaces, will not always end at the end of a word.

'Some persons object to the dividing of words at all in printing, as being unnecessary and displeasing to the eye; but then they must sacrifice all regularity of spacing, which is still worse, and gives the appearance of bad workmanship . . . I would recommend that a compositor should make each give a little way to the other, always preserving such a uniformity in spacing that there should be no glaring disproportion in different lines' [Savage41, p. 198].[10]

'Without doubt, words always appear better unbroken, but the breaking of words may not be so unsightly as the breaking up of a general uniformity of the spacing between words. To avoid divisions that may be offensive, the compositor may have to hair-space one line and em-quad the next line. He may make a worse division in the lines following that he has to overrun [*i.e.* re-set as a consequence of avoiding a bad word-break in an earlier line]. He may unintentionally produce the irregular up-curving gaps of white across lines, known as hounds'-teeth, which are more offensive to the reader than any strangeness of division' [De Vinne01, p. 139].

---

[10]This is essentially what TeX's paragraph-formatting algorithm aims to achieve.

It is clear that the manuals' authors, and De Vinne in particular, see the achievement of optically even interword spacing as very important indeed to the reader's comprehension of a text. The conflict between this requirement and the requirement for acceptable word division explains the amount of space devoted to the latter topic, both in the compositors' manuals and in publishers' style guides (*cf.* [Chicago82]).

There are two rival principles for word division in English: etymology and pronunciation. Hart, while discouraging word division in general, prefers etymology:

> 'Divide according to etymology, where this is obvious . . .
> Where etymological composition is not obvious, divide according to pronunciation' [Hart67, p. 13].

De Vinne finds etymology unsatisfactory, on the grounds that compositors should not be expected to be expert in Greek or Latin; but he cannot wholeheartedly recommend an alternative:

> 'The system which seems to have the most supporters in the United States is that which permits the division of a word on the emphasized syllable . . .
> 'No system of division known to the writer is so entirely satisfactory as to command general obedience' [De Vinne01, pp. 129 – 130].

A more recent authority comes down squarely for pronunciation [McIntosh90].

Whatever principle they recommend, all the manuals agree that the objective in dividing a word is to avoid break-points which disguise the identity of the divided word, or mislead the reader about its meaning by producing fragments which have inappropriate meanings of their own.

Delimiting compositional environments in text
In the era of hand composition, recognizing the boundaries of compositional environments, and knowing the rules that applied within them, was part of the compositor's task.

'When he meets with proper Names of Persons or Places he [*i.e.* the compositor] *Sets* them in *Italick*, if the Series of his *Matter* be *Set* in *Roman* . . . and *Sets* the first *Letter* with a *Capital*, or as the Person or Place he finds the purpose of the Author to dignifie, all *Capitals*; but then, if conveniently he can, he will *Set* a *Space* between every *Letter*, and two or three before and after that Name, to make it shew more Graceful and Stately'. [Moxon83, p 216].

The purpose of rules of composition

Rules of composition are intended to aid the reader's comprehension of a text by preventing the occurrence of inappropriate visual features in its realization.

This is the objective which underlies all the recommendations in the compositors' manuals, even when these seem at first sight to have only an aesthetic justification. Every feature of the visual structure of an actual document is an element of the scheme by which the document encodes the meaning of its author's message [Southall88, pp. 41 – 42]. If the information from one element of the encoding scheme conflicts with information from other elements, the overall encoding of the message becomes ambiguous. The reader has to make an effort, more or less conscious depending on the extent of the ambiguity, to recover the message's meaning by evaluating the relative contributions of the conflicting elements in its encoding.

In the Heideggerian terms used by Winograd and Flores [Winograd & Flores87, ch. 3], a well-composed document is ready-to-hand for the reader. The author's meaning flows through the visual content and structure of the marks in the document, but the marks themselves are not present to the reader. When the visual encoding of the message is ambiguous, the document becomes present-at-hand in the reader's world. The marks on the page appear to the reader *as marks*, with properties and relationships whose significance for the author's meaning has to be elucidated. It is the purpose of rules of composition to avoid breakdowns of this kind by ensuring that the visual encoding of the message is consistent, both within a document and from one document to another within a particular genre.

Rules of composition in present-day document production

Justifying text

Knuth's descriptions of the mechanism used by his T_EX system for justifying a paragraph of continuous text illustrate the number and scope of the rules and parameters which a computer-based document formatting system needs to carry out this task [Knuth84, ch. 12, 14].

It can be quite difficult to discover the content of the rules used by some other systems:

> 'To make the lines the same length [in justified text],
> Microsoft Word puts as many words on a line as will fit, and
> then it inserts additional space between the words to make
> the line end exactly at the right margin' [Microsoft88, p. 169].

Here the content of the spacing rules for justification and the values of their parameters are buried in the meanings given to *fit*, *inserts* and *additional* by the formatting program. These in turn are buried in the program's source code, which is inaccessible, so that the user can neither predict nor affect the behaviour of the system.

In T_EX, all the parameters of the rules for justification are accessible to the (expert) user, so that the system allows spacing rules to be defined and implemented which are comparable in content to those of the traditional technology. Unlike a human compositor, though, T_EX cannot deal explicitly with visual structure. In particular, the width of a fixed space cannot be set to a given proportion of the width of the interword spaces in the row in which it occurs. Hence De Vinne's rule for adjusting the widths of the spaces after commas and abbreviations so as to equalize the appearing spaces within a sentence cannot be implemented in T_EX.

Delimiting compositional environments

T_EX and its derivatives are unusual among present-day systems in that they have two sets of explicitly-defined rules of composition, one of which is intended for setting mathematics [Knuth84, ch. 16 – 19 and Appendix G]. The environments within which the rules for mathematical composition apply are marked by special delimiters in the virtual document, independently of the markup which labels its components as sections, subsections and so on.

The T_EXbook also describes several environments within which the user has to insert specific instructions into the text of a document in order to override the spacing rules which the system would otherwise apply. These implicitly delimited environments broadly correspond with the small-scale compositional environments of the traditional technology. They include proper names, within which the spaces between initials are marked to prevent them breaking over the end of a line [Knuth84, p. 73]; titles and abbreviations, with normal interword spaces placed after full points which T_EX would otherwise consider to be at the ends of sentences [*ibid.*, p. 74]; and nested quotation marks, separated by fixed amounts of space [*ibid.*, p. 5].

With present-day systems other than T_EX, procedural markup of this kind is discouraged [*cf.* Goldfarb81]. The purpose of the markup in a virtual document is to indicate the boundaries of content objects in the text. Compositional environments are not delimited as such; they are identifiable only if their boundaries happen to coincide with those of content objects. Thus, whatever the capabilities of the formatting system, it may be difficult to incorporate in a computer-formatted actual document the fine detail of visual structure which could have been achieved in the traditional technology, if the content structure of the virtual document is not marked up in a corresponding degree of detail.

Compositional environments in database publishing
Latterner and Woolf have described how the text of the mathematics abstracts journal *Mathematical Reviews* is built up by combining material submitted by reviewers with bibliographic information from a database [Latterner & Woolf89]. The result of this operation is a generically-marked-up virtual document with a very elaborate content structure. The markup in the document is extraordinarily detailed, so that delimiters can be found in it to correspond with the boundaries of almost all the components of the text which, in the traditional technology, would have been recognized as discrete compositional environments.

Thus, taking a theoretical view, the task of redesigning the typography of *Mathematical Reviews*, in which the present writer was engaged, consisted of identifying compositional environments in the journal text; locating their boundaries in the virtual document; defining appropriate rules of composition for them; and implementing the rules by modifying the TEX macros with which the document was formatted.[11] The change of typeface family from Computer Modern to Times, which was part of the same redesign, was in many ways secondary to this aspect of the work.

Conclusions

The distinction between graphic and visual structure has been discussed elsewhere [Southall89]. In the terms of that discussion, the task of a document formatting system is to give to an actual document a graphic structure such that its visual structure provides the reader with an accurate and consistent encoding of the content and content structure of its author's message.

Section 3 of the present paper discusses a few of the rules which were developed in the era of hand composition to perform this task satisfactorily.[12] While some of the rules, such as those which dictate where to add or remove space in an almost-justified line, have been overtaken by technology, others have not; and it is worth considering what would be required to implement them in a present-day system.

Visual structure

Mittelbach and Rowley point out that the way in which a content object in an actual document is formatted should depend on its visual as well as its logical context [Mittelbach & Rowley92]. The logical context of the object can be determined by parsing the content structure of the document. Its visual context is a consequence of its graphic context, which can be described (in principle, at any rate) in terms of the metric relationships between the marks on the display surface in the neighbourhood of the object in question. Information about these relationships is available from the formatting system's output: hence Mittelbach and Rowley's formatting paradigm can be seen as being realizable in principle on a system whose capabilities are no greater than those of the present day. However, its realization also depends on a

[11] The original macros were written by Patrick D. F. Ion, without whose unstinted help the redesign would not have been possible.
[12] The rules for spacing around punctuation marks, in particular, deserve much fuller treatment than they have been given here.

formalized understanding of the relationships between the graphic structure of documents and their visual structure. Mittelbach and Rowley suggest that such an understanding might be modelled using expert-systems techniques. To borrow a phrase from Pohl and Kornbluth's science-fiction classic, they do not exactly deny, and neither do they dwell on, the difficulties of this approach.[13]

Content structure and semantic structure

The compositor's objective in defining the graphic structure of a text is to produce an accurate and consistent visual realization of its content structure. The rules in the manuals are prescriptions for doing this within the constraints imposed by a particular technology.

Generally speaking, the content structure of the text is not described in detail in the manuscript from which the compositor works. Markup in the traditional technology serves primarily to resolve ambiguities which result from the limited graphic capability of the systems with which manuscripts are produced. Thus headings which have similar visual structures in a typescript are marked as being at different levels in the content structure of the text [Kaufmann78, pp. 22, 23], or greek and roman letters are distinguished in a mathematical manuscript [Chaundy 54, pp. 66 - 68]. It is taken for granted that the compositor will form an idea of the content structure of the text from an understanding of its semantic structure, and will go on to evaluate different possible arrangements of the marks in the actual document so as to optimize the accuracy and consistency with which the content structure is encoded.

Present-day document formatting systems are unable to interpret the semantic structure of a text in this sense. The only notion of content structure they are able to form is the one conveyed to them by the information in the document type description, which defines the set of objects in the structure and the relationships which exist between them, and by the markup in the virtual document itself. As was suggested in section 4.3 above, this explicit markup is very often much less detailed than the implicit markup which a compositor is able to discern in the text of a manuscript.

[13]Frederik Pohl & C. M. Kornbluth, *The space merchants*. London: Heinemann, 1955.

The compositor, however, discovers the semantic structure of a text, at least in part, by parsing the sequence of characters and spaces which the manuscript contains. While it is important not to underestimate the significance of the other factors which go to form the compositor's understanding, it seems possible that the kinds of approach to the analysis of content which have already been used to produce automatic spelling-checkers and grammar-checkers might be extended to provide automatic detection of content structure at the sentence level. Some theoretical steps have already been taken in this direction [Nunberg88].

Acknowledgement

The research on compositors' practice reported in this paper was begun in the System Sciences Laboratory at Xerox Palo Alto Research Center, and was partly funded by the Nippon Telegraph and Telephone Corporation. I am grateful to David Levy for making this work possible.

This paper was first published in 'E.P. 92', editors; Vanoirbeek C and Coray G, and is reproduced here by kind permission of Cambridge University Press.

References

[**Brun**25] M. A. Brun, *Manuel pratique et abrégé de la typographie française*, Paris, Firmin Didot, 1825.

[**Carter**69] Harry Carter, *A view of early typography*. Oxford: Clarendon Press, 1969.

[**Chaundy**54] T. W. Chaundy, P. R. Barrett, and C. Batey, *The printing of mathematics*, London, Oxford University Press, 1954.

[Chicago82] *The Chicago manual of style* (13th edition), Chicago, University of Chicago Press, 1982.

[DeVinne01] T. L. De Vinne, *Correct composition,* New York, Century, 1901.

[DeVinne04] T. L. De Vinne, *Modern methods of book composition,* New York, Century, 1904.

[Fournier66] Simon-Pierre Fournier, *Manuel typographique.* Paris: Fournier, 1764 (vol. I), 1766 (vol. II).

[Goldfarb81] C. F. Goldfarb, "A generalized approach to document markup", *ACM SIGPLAN Notices,* vol. 16 no. 6, June 1981, pp. 68–73.

[Hart67] *Hart's rules for compositors and readers at the University Press, Oxford,* (37th edition), Oxford, Oxford University Press, 1967.

[Jennett64] S. Jennett, *The making of books* (3rd edition), London, Faber, 1964.

[Kaufmann87] W. Kaufmann, *One book/five ways,* Los Altos, Ca., Kaufmann, 1978.

[Knuth84] D. E. Knuth, *The T$_E$Xbook,* Reading, Mass., Addison-Wesley, 1984.

[Knuth84] D. E. Knuth, *Computer Modern typefaces (Computers & typesetting,* vol. E), Reading, Mass., Addison-Wesley, 1986.

[Lamport86] L. Lamport, LAT$_E$X: *a document preparation system,* Reading, Mass., Addison-Wesley, 1986.

[Latterner89] D. C. Latterner and W. B Woolf, "T$_E$X at *Mathematical Reviews",* TUGboat, vol. 10 no. 4, December 1989, pp. 639–654.

[**Mandel**78] Ladislas Mandel, "Il nuovo carattere Galfra per gli elenchi telefonici italiani", *Graphicus*, vol. 9, 1978.

[**McIntosh**90] R. McIntosh, *Hyphenation,* Bradford, Computer Hyphenation Ltd, 1990.

[**Microsoft**88] *Microsoft Word for Windows user's reference,* Microsoft Corporation, 1988.

[**Mittelbach**92] F. Mittelbach and C. Rowley, "The pursuit of quality: How can automated typesetting achieve the highest standards craft typography?", these proceedings.

[**Moxon**83] J. Moxon, *Mechanick exercises on the whole art of printing* (1683). Edited by H. Davis and H. Carter (2nd edition). Oxford, Oxford University Press, 1962; New York, Dover, 1978.

[**Nunberg**88] G. Nunberg, *The linguistics of punctuation*, Report no. P88–00142, System Sciences Laboratory, Xerox Palo Alto Research Center, 1988.

[**Rubinstein**88] Richard Rubinstein, *Digital typography – an introduction to type and composition for computer system design.* Reading, Mass.: Addison-Wesley, 1988.

[**Savage**41] W. Savage, *Dictionary of the art of printing,* London, Longman, Brown, Green & Longmans, 1841.

[**Seybold**79] J. W. Seybold, *Fundamentals of modern photocomposition,* Media, Pa., Seybold, 1979.

[**Simon**68] H. Simon, *Introduction to printing,* London, Faber, 1968.

[**Smith**55] J. Smith, *The printer's grammar,* London, Owen, 1755.

Southall88] R. Southall, "Visual structure and the transmission of meaning", in J. C. van Vliet (ed.), *Document manipulation and typography,* Cambridge University Press, 1988, pp. 35–45.
[**Southall**89] R. Southall, "Interfaces between the designer and the

[**Southall**89] R. Southall, "Interfaces between the designer and the document", J. André, R. Furuta & V. Quint (eds.), *Structured documents*, Cambridge University Press, 1989, pp. 119–131.

[**Tschichold**67] J. Tschichold, *Asymmetric typography,* New York, Reinhold, 1967.

[**USGPO**62] United States Government Printing Office, *Theory and practice of composition,* Washington, D. C., Government Printing Office, 1962.

[**Winograd**87] T. Winograd and F. Flores, *Understanding computers and cognition,* Reading, Mass., Addison-Wesley, 1987.

PART 2

TYPOGRAPHIC CHOICES – LATIN AND OTHER ALPHABETS

Digital hebrew in a monolingual world

ARI DAVIDOW SPECIALIST IN NON–LATIN TYPEFACES, INTERNET: ari@well.sf.ca.us.

'We not only need to develop tools for working with single languages in all the complexities of their traditional forms. We also need to develop tools and forms that facilitate the presentation of languages together.'

Spoiled for choice

ELWYN AND MICHAEL BLACKER

With the graphics tools and technology available today the possibilities for manipulating letter forms or creating new alphabets are endless. The results, however, are not always successful and do we really need even more alphabets

ARI DAVIDOW

Digital Hebrew in a Monolingual World

I'm going to write a few words about a subject dear to my heart. This is the idea that computers could open new doors for all of us who speak languages other than English. I'm going to focus on the language that has been most familiar to me other than English, which is Hebrew. I don't mean to slight other languages or other alphabets, but each time I sit down to try to write about the issue of using computers to work with all languages in general I find myself drowning in the multitude of stories and issues specific to each one. To paraphrase O. Henry, there are dozens of alphabets, and in each one, hundreds of thousands of stories. So, let us adopt a paradigm and accept that while putting Hebrew characters onto a computer screen and editing them poses unique challenges, much the same can be said of any alphabet. At the same time, we can get a sense of what it means to merge the modern arts of computer magic with the ancient arts of calligraphy and type by examining this one specific alphabet.

We needn't stray so far as Hebrew to get a sense of the potential of computers and written language. Nor do we need to consider Hebrew to realize that our use of computers to represent the written language – even English – has yet to approach its potential. Consider these two facts. There is an international standard for the Latin letters called ASCII. It consists of all 26 letters of the alphabet, upper and lower case. It contains all of the punctuation marks found on the common typewriter keyboard, and there are even a few special symbols common to computer programs. There are no ligatures. None, whatsoever. ASCII defines 128 characters and codes (including a teletype bell code to alert operators).

Gutenberg's fonts included some 400 characters. Gutenberg didn't even consider numbers, copyright signs, currency symbols. Nor did he have the foresight to include characters such as the backslash ('\') so important to programmers. And he still came up with 400 characters. When I therefore digress to note that classical Arabic typography requires some 330-odd characters, we find ourselves marvelling not that Arabic is complicated, but wondering how early typographers sufficed with a mere 330 or 340 sorts!

I note this paradox not to lament the simplification of our alphabet nor to bemoan the fact that users of IBM-compatible computers to this day have no access to even the most common of ligatures, 'fl' or 'fi.' I think that it is more important to accept the fact that, to a point, the art of typography has also been a science of mass production. And, common to the needs of mass production, we have simplified the process along the way.

The typewriter, which served as the basis for the keyboard we use to type letters onto the computer, completes this simplification to an alarming degree. When I was young, it was unheard of for a typewriter to devote a special key to the number one. In typing class we all learned that the lower case 'ell' was appropriate, just as we learned that a capital 'oh' was as good as a zero and saved our fingers from reaching up to that far off row where the numbers are displayed. Now, here's where the magic begins. When I was a child and we spoke both Hebrew and English around the house, we had only an English typewriter. We never procured one for Hebrew. This meant that by the time I was in high school and had learned to type, my formal papers in English were always neatly typewritten. Papers written for religious school, however, could never be other than handwritten. For some, this would have been a pleasure, but I have crabby, stunted, wandering handwriting. For me, it was torture; and the handwritten page lacks the authority of one that is neatly typewritten. Partly as a consequence, it was not until the computer age was sufficiently advanced for me to encounter programs that enabled me to type in Hebrew that I began to study the language seriously, to begin writing in the language at all.

As I frequently remind myself as I stare at an office spilling over with computers and their detritus, I only got interested in these new machines to write more easily. All of the hacking and programming came about only because these marvellous machines were engineered in such a way as to make it difficult for me to accomplish that most basic of tasks: to type in Hebrew, write, compose, muse, search, hash out words … in English and Hebrew.

The Art of Hebrew Printing

I have been working with Hebrew for some ten years now. The more I learn, the more I find myself consulting the old masters. One of the most interesting things that quickly becomes clear is that there is more to Hebrew typography than letters. Consider, for instance, that staple of illuminated manuscripts: the illustrated drop cap. There is no such thing in ancient Hebrew manuscript. Instead, an entire word is illustrated. Letters are ephemeral. It's true that each letter has mystic significance, but the joy of Hebrew is not in the individual letters, but in the words created by the letters.

Here, let me illustrate for a moment with a story. One of the Hebrew letters is called the 'yud'. It is the smallest of letters, a short squiggle. In Yiddish, the word 'yud' also means 'Jew'. Further, know that among the common names for God in Hebrew, the shortest may be a word composed of two 'yuds'.

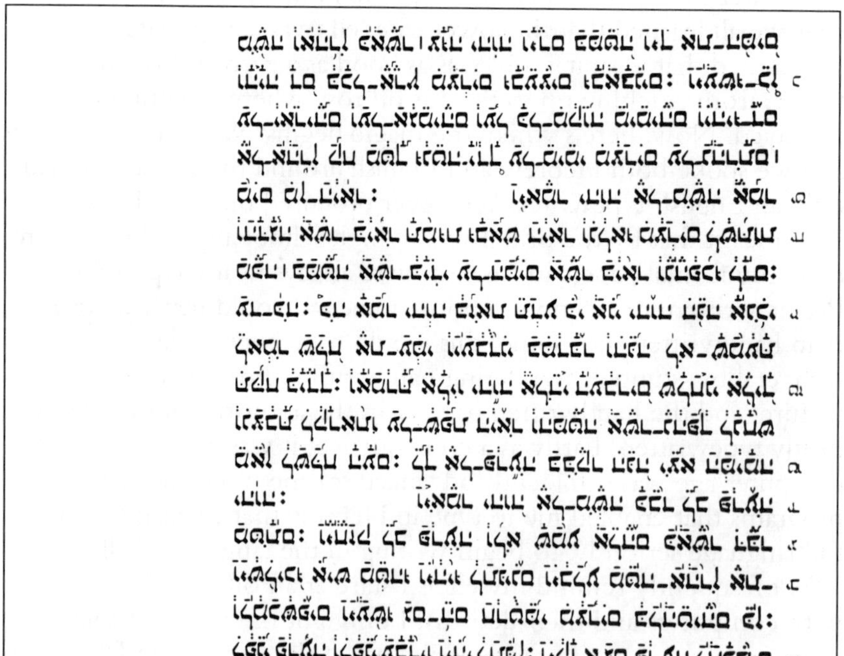

Figure 1

Page from the Koren Bible. This is the most beautiful example of modern Hebrew typography. After the basic pages were printed, Koren and a team of calligraphers spent three years writing in the vowel points and calligraphic characters (the diacriticals above and below the basic characters). We'll know that Hebrew can really be done on computers when this page can be duplicated by professional computer composition software.

A famous preacher was once asked to deliver a one-minute sermon. 'Well' says the preacher, 'consider the "yud". By itself, it is just a letter, just as a person, by himself, is nothing of significance. In fact,' continues the preacher, 'if you take two 'yuds' and place them on a page, one above the other, you still have nothing. But if you place the two side by side, you have God.'

And there you have it. In traditional Hebrew manuscript there are no drop caps. Instead, the scribes would take an entire word as the text for their illustration. This is a small point, but to us it connotes much.

By the same token, Hebrew doesn't really hyphenate. In the Latin alphabet, we differentiate between consonants and vowels. There is no visual differentiation between the two: it's just that some letters are one, and a few the other. In Hebrew, the alphabet consists only of consonants. The vowels, when necessary, are entered as diacritical marks, usually below the consonants. Early Hebrew printers had a difficult time of it. They did not have the flexibility of calligraphy. (Although calligraphers still use elongated forms of some letters to aid the justification of lines.) Instead, they would create both elongated and tiny letters, and use one or the other. In some cases, they would fill space with part of a word and then repeat it in *toto* on the following line. Or they would place a letter backwards to fill up the space. From my own perspective, such practices lack much in the way of both aesthetic and readability, but there you have it. To this day, hyphenation in Hebrew is problematic.

Hebrew Vowels

A few moments ago I mentioned Hebrew vowels. These are the small diacritical marks that guide the pronunciation of words. In many cases they are considered superfluous. Examination of a modern Israeli newspaper will betray little evidence of their use. Calligraphers, of course, could place these marks where they best fit the aesthetic of the word and character. Early printers were limited and often placed the vowels awkwardly. It's not hard to understand the problem: the printer carefully lays out a page, revises it, lays it out again, and then moves all of the vowels to align properly.

The problem has defied ordinary technology to this day. One of the most common complaints of users of modern Hebrew computer software is that either the software does not support the placement of vowels at all, or that the placement is ugly. It's not a problem that is much easier for the professionals either. The most beautiful printed Hebrew Bible of this century was created by Koren in the middle of this century. He designed a beautiful typeface for the Hebrew consonants and had the Bible printed conventionally. He then spent three years, in secret, with a team of calligraphers inking the vowels and other diacritical marks onto the master proofs before offset printing the result.

For the sake of historical completeness, I should also note that in addition to eleven basic vowel symbols, there are a few dozen other marks that are placed above, below, and even inside the letters. Most users of modern Hebrew would just as soon forget that these marks exist. Their only use is in Bible studies. As it so happens, three or four million people speak modern Hebrew. They may actually be outnumbered by those whose interest in Hebrew lies precisely in its historical role as 'the language of the Bible'. So it goes.

Hebrew Italic

In addition to the unresolved question of mechanically setting the vowels and other diacriticals, there is an additional typographic challenge. What on earth is an appropriate Hebrew italic? In this case, there are both obvious answers and cultural answers. I bring this up not because there is a lack of cursive forms in old Hebrew printing, or because the cursive forms were used differently than the equivalent forms in English (usually, to save space). Somehow, we have lost Hebrew cursive. Not only does modern written Hebrew cursive bear even less resemblance to the traditional forms than, say, Palmer to Copperplate, but only one modern Hebrew typeface boasts an italic that is shaped by cursive forms. Instead, in slavish imitation of Latin forms, and heavily influenced by modern typographic ideas, the tendency is to slant the letterforms, just as is done with modern, primarily sans serif, forms of English.

That, of course, raises the question 'in which direction does Hebrew slant?' There is no unanimity among type designers as yet. Henri Friedlander, one of the deans of modern Hebrew

Figure 2
Newspaper ads are a
wonderful place to view
the hodgepodge of
alphabets and
letterforms as
commonly used. These
ads from an Israeli
newspaper live up to
the billing. Note that
type is slanted both to
the left and to the right
in two ads on the left-
hand side. Which
direction is correct?
There is no agreement
among Israeli
typographers or type
users.

typography, contends that all cursive styles slant the same way.
Cursive is always influenced by the way we hold the pen. Tzvi
Narkiss, one of Friedlander's contemporaries, avers with similar
assurance that just as Hebrew is written from right to left – the
opposite direction from that of English – so, too, must Hebrew
cursives slant in the opposite direction to English.

Aesthetically, the question should be moot. I find it instructive to
consider the notes of Henri Friedlander, the creator of Hadassah –
considered, deservedly, one of the best modern Hebrew text
forms.

In describing his attempt at a Hadassah italic, Friedlander found
himself most displeased with the results achieved by slanting the
letters. He commented that it was impossible to distinguish easily
between the slanted form in his test proof and the upright form. I
might add that I have often noted this problem with Latin faces
such as Melior. In the end, Friedlander deferred the idea of a
Hadassah italic, and the face was released in text and bold upright
forms only.

This hasn't inhibited the use of slanted type in the least.
Computers make it too easy to ignore the wisdom of those who

created the type in the first place. But, almost without exception, no Hebrew typefaces currently on the market come with 'true' italics.

I have no explanation for this lack. I can point out that italic fell much into disfavour in Hebrew printed manuscripts over the centuries, but I do not know why. The fact is, however, that one can open the page of any Israeli newspaper and see type slanted both to the left and to the right – often in facing advertisements. And, with the exception of Ismar David's wonderful 'David' face (unique not only in the fact that there is an associated cursive, but also in the fact that it is a true cursive), no modern Hebrew type designer has created a cursive font designed to work with an accompanying roman.

The monolingual computer

So here is the situation. We have the modern computer, suitable for desktop composition in any language (so long as it is English), with type of all shapes and sizes. The current edition of one word processor on my Macintosh will even allow me to incorporate video images into my documents. (Why? I don't know why. But an awful lot of people have told me they use the software solely because it has that ability – should they ever choose to use it.) I don't even want to talk about what happens when I try to type Hebrew using the program.

Early computer designers imposed limits that haunt us today. One such lack of prescience was to expect that computer programmers would only speak English. When they developed ASCII as a standard language so computers could communicate with each other, they based it on the standard American typewriter keyboard.

Now, let's talk some computerese. ASCII is what is known as a 7-bit code. There are 2^7 characters, or a total of 128. The ASCII standard is understood by almost all computers in the world. Better yet, most modern computers think in terms of bytes, or 8 bits at a time. This doubles the amount of characters in a font to 2^8, or 256 characters.

If you look at the character charts for various modern computers, you will note that the first 128 characters, ASCII, are always the same. The next 128 characters are standard for IBM, or DEC, or

OPPOSITE:
Figure 3
IBM PC Hebrew Encoding: This shows how Hebrew is slipped into the standard IBM character set. Note that only the basic 27 letterforms are included. The rest of the characters are just as they would be for users of the standard English IBM system.

Figure 4
Kivun Character Set: This is a "complete" Hebrew character set as proposed by an Israeli computer manufacturer. There are four groups of characters: The basic 27 letterform, the usual modifications of those 27 letterforms, some ligatures and extended characters, and the diacritical marks used to mark vowels and cantorial symbols. For all of its length, the set does not address the needs of modern Hebrew. it does not include modern israeli quote marks, some modern Hebrew characters used to indicate sounds foreign to Hebrew, nor does it include the Israeli currency symbol.

Macintosh, or Apple II, but bear little resemblance to each other. On the original IBM PC, the extra codes were used for the most common European accented characters, line-drawing characters, and some important mathematical symbols. The graphically-oriented Mac didn't need line-drawing characters, so a few more European characters were added, along with some of the more important typographic symbols: em and en dashes, some ligatures, some dipthongs, plus a few international currency symbols, and the like.

Cramming the alphabet

For people using languages other than English, that bonus of 128 characters provides a place to create national standards for other alphabets and languages: German, Russian, Greek, even Hebrew. At least, you could work in those languages with limitations similar to those facing typographers working in English: you had your

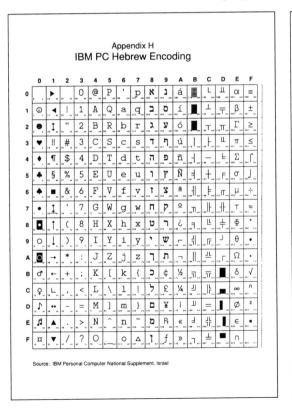

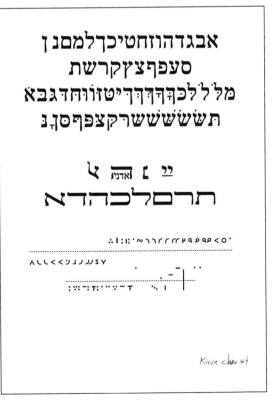

basic alphabet, but never enough characters to do sophisticated typography.

Unfortunately, the 256-character system doesn't really work. Some languages have far more characters than there are keys – Japanese, Chinese and Korean, for example, each use about 10,000 characters (and I have heard higher estimates for 'proper' typography in any of these languages). Many languages, especially Arabic or the languages of India, require complex systems to combine characters. As I mentioned earlier, classical Arabic requires more than 330 characters. It is only recently that Arabic was simplified sufficiently for sane, if unaesthetic, keyboard composition. But if the characters needed for a given language don't fit on a regular typewriter keyboard, they also won't fit into the software limits imposed by the way our computers work.

Obviously there have been workarounds, but more questions arise. What constitutes the appropriate and reasonable set of characters for a given language? How should the keys on the keyboard be laid out? Even in the case of Hebrew, with its 27 basic characters and no separate cases, there are those 11 vowel diacriticals, a few special ligatures for Yiddish or Judesmo, and a couple of dozen additional marks.

Beyond that, one need only look at the rapidly changing map of Europe to realize that in the best of circumstances, most of the world cannot get by with computers that awkwardly provide the use of two languages any more than they can with our common, linguistically-impaired, monolingual models. The same Tel Aviv office that shares files in English with its New York office may need to do the same in Arabic, or Russian, or Ethiopic for the local population.

The sad state of the art

The challenge hasn't gone unanswered. There are many PC-based word processing programs that work with many languages and alphabets. Some are limited to two languages (English and Hebrew, for example); others, such as the versatile MultiLingual Scholar (Gamma Productions), tackle dozens. In each case, the programs were designed independently. This means that formatted text cannot be exchanged between such programs in the same way that, say, a WordPerfect file in English can be converted to a format understood by Microsoft Word. For many of these programs there are even usable laser fonts available, specific to each individual program.

Because there are no universal standards for characters in languages other than English, there has been a corresponding disincentive to create high quality fonts to work with these programs. A company would have to invest significantly to address a minor market; not only must unique printer drivers (the code with which the word processor talks to the printer) be written for each word processor, but the sets of characters, the keyboard layouts, and the order in which the characters are stored must be customized in each case.

On the Mac side, Apple has taken the lead in working with different languages and alphabets. It has released more than 30 separate versions of its current operating system, each localized for a particular language and/or alphabet. The developer's CD-ROM from Apple includes systems for countries ranging from Iceland to Korea to Japan. So far, these systems are only available in the countries where such systems would be used, or, for developers, through Apple. The Japanese version of the Macintosh operating system became available commercially in the United States on a limited – and costly – basis in 1991. Other foreign language systems will also become available in time.

Computing almost good enough 'for the rest of us'

Apple has been developing these foreign operating systems for several years. They continue to improve, and yet, they are no better than adequate. Following the lead of other manufacturers, Apple has taken a dual-language approach. Where other computer system manufacturers limited localization efforts to using the ASCII upper 128 characters to add extra characters, Apple went further and actually built routines into the Mac operating system to facilitate working with different languages.

Users of the French system pop back and forth between ASCII (English) and French by pressing a key combination or clicking an icon. In French mode, a different spelling dictionary may be selected. The keyboard layout changes. The way that dates will appear or long numbers are expressed on a spreadsheet will follow European conventions – even your currency symbol will change automatically. If your second language is Hebrew or Arabic, these routines understand that when you are working in either of these languages, text moves from right to left across the page. Clicking the icon to work in English causes the text to begin flowing again from left to right.

Like many things on the Mac, these dual-language systems are easy to use. The smarts are built into the Mac operating system as the 'Script Manager', where a 'script' refers to all of the house-keeping that a computer needs to track when you switch languages.

As it turns out, most programs on the market ignore the Script Manager. Apple's effort was noble, but the routines were crude, bug-ridden and slow. So, even if you are using a dual-language operating system, programs may or may not understand what is happening. Using Microsoft Word or Aldus PageMaker with Hebrew or Arabic can be an extraordinarily uncomfortable experience. The American version of QuarkXpress will immediately bomb if it encounters resources from any systems other than the standard American system. (That's right: Load a font designed to work with Apple's Arabic system in QuarkXPress, and prepare to reboot your computer.) Both Aldus and Quark have released customized Japanese versions of their products (Quark also offers a European version of XPress, but you'll have to shell out thousands of dollars for it). In the main, these programs follow the lead of PC products: the specific routines are unique to the individual programs and don't work with other languages.

Publishing and word processing programs on the Macintosh that follow Apple guidelines do exist. They're hard to find, but they work. The Hebrew version of Paragon Concepts' Nisus (already an extraordinary word processor in English) can be used, on the sly, to do basic work in many of Apple's foreign language systems. There's also a Japanese-specific version of Nisus called SoloWriter. MicroMacro, based in New Jersey, USA, has some less well-known products for publishing and word processing (AllPage and AllScript, respectively) and are entirely Script Manager compatible. MicroMacro products will even work flawlessly with customized conglomerations of Apple's foreign language scripts. One of the company's favourite demonstrations is to combine the linguistic abilities of several alphabets and create documents which skip, effortlessly, from Japanese to Arabic to Hebrew to Thai to English.

If you don't need to exchange files with other computers, there are other alternatives to working with foreign languages on the Macintosh. Two American-based companies – Linguist's Software and Ecological Linguistics – provide a wide variety of fonts with different alphabets, and phonetic and technical symbols. These fonts are designed for scholars and do not tend to be of highest quality or aesthetic appeal. All will suffice for word processing and all of them will work with the linguistically-impaired Macword processor of your choice. You don't even need foreign language editions of the Mac operating system. Both companies provide excellent service.

For those especially attuned to the changes in Europe, the Casady & Greene cornucopia of fonts are pleasant alternatives. (A spokeperson for the company reports that at one point, their Cyrillic "Glasnost" collection outsold all of the company's English-language fonts.)

The 64,000-character future

At some point we'll need to be able to work comfortably with many languages in a standard way. Our economy is global. Europe is now, technically, one country, and few of us will want to go back to the limited neighbourhoods of yesteryear. It isn't enough to have computers that are multimedial, multimodal or multitasking. Our computers, like most people in the world, need to be multilingual. This will probably not take place so long as computers are forced to limit fonts to 256 characters.

Some panaceas are on the horizon. One is a new character set called Unicode, announced in February 1991. Unicode simply doubles the number of bits used to define a unique character. The result is a vast set of 65,000 two-byte characters. This means that a unique code can be assigned to all common characters in all languages. The code also includes a wide variety of technical and illustrative symbols. Unfortunately, Unicode is to multilingual typography as ASCII is to English typography. Not everything is there.

Despite these limitations, American computer manufacturers and software designers have accepted Unicode as the best way to create computers for the rest of us. Both Apple's "Worldscript" extensions to its current Macintosh operating system (System 7), and Microsoft's recently-demonstrated Windows NT product, both due in Fall 1992, are said to support Unicode.

In the context of needing something standard that works for most people, Unicode is certainly a giant step in the right direction. But I have to wonder. Even in the case of Hebrew, a relatively simple alphabet, Unicode does not include all of the characters that a typographer or calligrapher would want. Like ASCII, Unicode provides a useful pidgin alphabet that enables basic standard communication. But we're not talking about typewriters. We aren't limited by physical keys. Why can't computers address communication in ways that go beyond the basic? There is a competing ISO standard under development called ISO 10646 but, to date, there is no agreement among the scholars involved in its preparation as to the final character sets for many languages. A ray of hope appeared in July 1992 when it was announced that Unicode would somehow merge with ISO 10646, resulting in a Unicode, version 1.1 with a greatly enlarged set of characters. I look forward to seeing the revised character set.

At some point, we typographers are going to have to step in. 'Okay,' we'll say. 'It's fine that we have these basic characters for all languages. Now, here is how we'll use these magical machines to set type properly.' To me it makes a most powerful argument for typographers to become involved with computers. Our interest doesn't lie only in the wonderful variety of tools for creating type or laying the type out. Ultimately, we have a lot of work to do in developing ways, using the computer, to abandon the mechanical simplicity of modern typesetting devices and to make it possible for languages and alphabets to evolve once again into complexity.

Digital Hebrew in a multilingual world
In all of this talk about computers and basic Hebrew I have neglected one of the main issues which arises once one works with many languages together: what sorts of design criteria affect working with two or more languages in the same document?

Between Hebrew and English there is such a profound difference between the alphabets, that I didn't really notice there was a problem until I began working with Russian and English. Suddenly I realized that I had several versions of Times New Roman Cyrillic, but no type that felt … Russian. It is a modern affectation that everything should look the same. At the entrance to the United Nations there is a wall greeting all comers in all of the languages spoken in those halls. And each and every alphabet is designed in a geometric face resembling Avant Garde.

This is truly awful. Perhaps one can accept it when so many languages are merged together on one wall. Perhaps in that one case the cacophony created by so many different styles would be overwhelming. But in normal usage there is nothing aesthetic, or particularly useful for communications in making languages look alike. On the contrary, when working with different languages – even when working with languages that are relatively similar in appearance, such as English and French – a designer should want to make it easy for the eye to distinguish between the languages.

When one insists on making languages look the same, one finds oneself with solutions similar to that used at the UN. One discovers that the only way to create parallel styles is to move away from traditional forms and into modern, simplified forms such as Avant Garde, or sans serif types in general. This is obviously not something that works well for large bodies of text, even were the design goal laudable. There is also something not to be said in favour of abandoning the complexity of traditional forms.

It is much harder to find complementary designs, especially when working with different alphabets, than to make one design fit all. Yet, it is simply not appropriate to do otherwise. One of my most treasured visual experiences was discovering a polyglot Psalter printed by Pietro Paolo Porro, printed in Genoa in 1516. Porro artfully arranged Hebrew, Greek, Latin, and Arabic with a skill that has seldom been matched. In modern times, the reader will delight in the work of American artist Ben Shahn. In particular, Shahn created several pieces using his graffiti-based English letters with a rougher, equally effusive Hebrew alphabet. In no way are the two alphabets alike, other than in spirit. Yet, in Shahn's hands, they are a delight to read.

When I do multilingual design I find myself mixing serif and sans serif (if the languages are based on the Latin alphabet), even, occasionally, roman and italic. The eye must focus less on surface similarities (does it all look like Times Roman?), and instead focus on shapes: is the equivalent height of the letters similar? Do the curves express themselves in similar, or complementary ways? I try

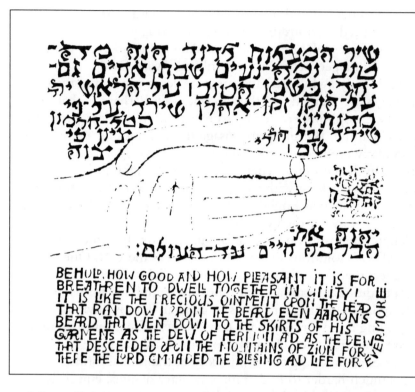

Figure 5
Ben Shahn's Alphabet of Creation and Polyglot English.
Ben Shahn was the modern master of alphabets and lettering. In this piece he combined his standard Hebrew and English alphabets to perfect effect. Note how the shapes complement each other despite the surface disparities.

to follow Shahn's approach of allowing the external shapes to be different and searching for a design in which the faces add up to something together which would not otherwise be achieved.

Each combination of alphabets poses different challenges. One of my favourites is posed by mixing a Latin-based language with one based on Cyrillic. On the surface, the two alphabets are quite similar. Indeed, the goal of Peter the Great, the Russian Tsar who shaped the modern Cyrillic alphabet, was to make the alphabet 'Western'. But the similarity in feel disappears the instant one strays from the upper case. Where the Latin alphabet uses a lower case derived from a different form of writing, the Cyrillic equivalent is based on the minuscule – small caps. Not only does this exacerbate the traditional translator's problem in which a paragraph of text almost always appears longer in translation, but the real width of text comprised of the same number of characters will always be wider. And in all events, the languages simply feel different. Why on earth, therefore, would a designer try to mask these differences

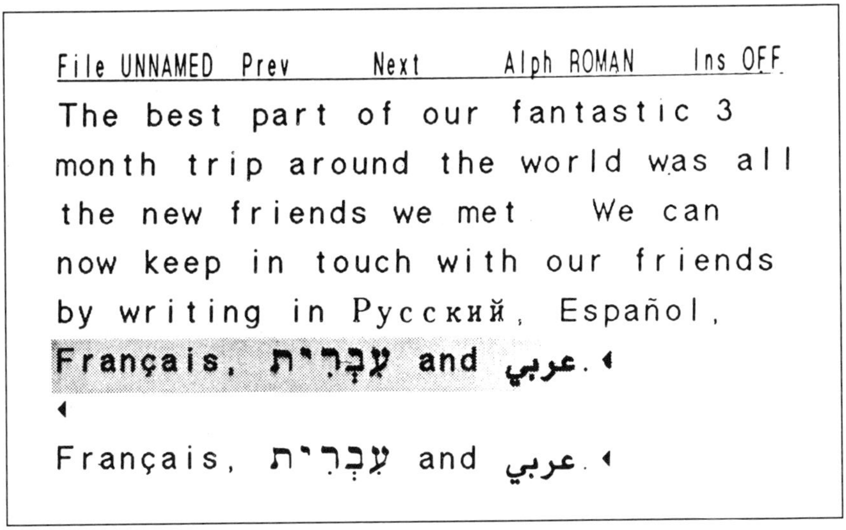

Figure 6
Screen display of a modern multilingual word processor.
This is an editing display from Multilingual Scholar, a popular, IBM-compatible-based multilingual editor. Note that while the screen display isn't terribly inviting, the user can work in several languages at once, viewing the characters properly as he or she is writing.

```
File UNNAMED  Prev      Next      Alph ROMAN    Ins OFF
The  best  part  of  our  fantastic  3
month  trip  around  the  world  was  all
the  new  friends  we  met    We  can
now  keep  in  touch  with  our  friends
by  writing  in  Русский,  Español,
Français,  עִבְרִית  and  عربي .  ◄

◄
Français,  עִבְרִית  and  عربي .  ◄
```

and make it harder for the reader to follow the text of a given language?

Hebrew poses a typical, albeit unique, set of challenges. Most of the characters are based around a block shape and there is no lower case. This means that, when mixed with Latin-based languages, the height of the Hebrew characters must be less than that of the Latin caps, yet significantly higher than the x-height. For maximum readability, columns of text in the two languages should start from a common visual point and flow outwards towards the margins of the page, away from each other. (For some reason, the opposite is often done, with the result that readers of polyglot text find their eyes straining with the difficulty of tracking back and forth. The problem is less acute when text is justified, but never disappears.)

Mixing Hebrew with Arabic poses an entirely different set of challenges. Both languages read from the same direction, but now we contrast the blockiness of traditional Hebrew forms with the flow of traditional Arabic. Once again, height must be adjusted between the two alphabets to deliver a consistent colour. And, once again, the styles of type must be carefully selected so that the two complement each other. This can be a challenge because there are few commercially available typefaces in either language. And, most usually, one sees the most common forms of each alphabet mixed together with no attempt at harmony. (I sometimes wonder if this is a case of art imitating life. If so, the implications of better Hebrew–Arabic design become rather staggering!)

Assuming that computer manufacturers realize the need for multilingual tools, this is the area of greatest challenge for typographers. We not only need to develop tools for working with single languages in all the complexities of their traditional forms, we also need to develop tools and forms that facilitate the presentation of languages together.

To me, this is the key to realizing the potential magic of computers. It will never be enough to put desktop composition tools into the hands of computer users who stick to one language. Imagine what happens when people can use computers to work in all languages of choice, and have the tools to do so aesthetically? We would finally have the tools to meet the modern age with the facility and grace that Porro met his in the sixteenth century.

After all, one of the mysteries of modern computers is why, if we can use them to display pictures in hundreds of thousands of colours, to incorporate speech and sound … even video…. how come we aren't using them to shape pages with the basic building blocks of written communication – the alphabet – in ways at least as aesthetic as those used by Gutenberg? Why aren't we demanding that these same computers facilitate written communication in all languages and alphabets? Give me Hebrew and Arabic in all their glory. Give me Czech and Hungarian and Tamil and Thai. Give me Armenian and Ethiopic and Korean; Devanagari, Icelandic, and even, give me a beautiful English. If I can't do it on a computer, I may as well return to letterpress. Or calligraphy. Sheesh.

ELWYN AND MICHAEL BLACKER

Spoiled for choice

In an article written in 1946, replying to a savage attack by Max Bill on his 'New Typography', Jan Tschichold wrote '. . . the technical principle of machine composition has not had the least influence on design methods. Machine composition imitates hand composition, the nearer the better . . . It is less flexible, not at all easier to handle than hand composition . . . it is more efficient, but in no way able to change materially the appearance of typography by means of some sort of "mechanical" law of its own.'

   Tschichold was, of course, writing about hot metal machine composition. Had he been writing about computer composition his reaction would, almost certainly, have been different. While recognising the dangers inherent in the ability to expand, contract and generally distort letter forms, he would have appreciated the enormous flexibility which computers give designers to fine-tune the detailed aspects of typographical composition.

Too many alphabets?
Fine typography should be healthier now than it has ever been. Combined with the greater flexibility, computers have reduced the cost of developing new type faces and, as a result, the range of faces available is enormous. Unfortunately, many of the 'revivals' of classical faces and many of the faces specially designed for the new technology are undistinguished or, worse, are distorted versions of elegant alphabets.

   Do we need even more alphabets? Are not type users already spoiled for choice? Frederic W. Goudy (who contributed 120 faces to the repertoire) said that 'the old fellows had forestalled all of our best ideas . . . My own feeling in regard to the endless reviving of old types is the same feeling I have toward dead and living literature: the new never transcends itself and is always imitative, never moving with the spontaneous energy that is indicative of freshness and originality.'

Instead of adding to the many thousands of alphabets already available, designers should concentrate on taking full advantage of the refinements which are now possible.

Technology, such as the Multiple Master font system, has 'axes' to alter the weight and width of an alphabet in small increments between two wide range bands and to alter 'style' by, for example, replacing slab serifs with wedge serifs or even removing serifs altogether. But the system can also – and this must surely be the most important of its features – amend the optical size to produce the most legible characters for a particular size of letter.

The thirty primary Multiple Master fonts from which almost infinite variations can be created.

The letters of the finest hot metal (and film) alphabets were drawn with care and precision and altered for different sizes to balance thick and thin strokes. Each letter was considered individually for *each* size in which it was to be made available. One has only to compare the different sizes of a traditional hot-metal face, such as Caslon Old Face, to see how significant those variations in letter forms were.

Fine typography *is* possible

The flexibility which was not available to the hand or machine typesetter imposes none of the mechanical restraints which were an integral part of good typographic design. As with photography, computer composition has become available to all at the touch of a button. What is apparent is that fine typography can only be produced by skilled designers with a mastery of the optical considerations. Sadly, those not trained in the use of hot metal composition with the restrictions it imposed – as for instance in the relationship of individual letters to each other, and even in the letter forms themselves – are less able to see the essential differences. The thrill of the new technology, with its apparently infinite possibilities and varieties, takes over.

The ability to fine-tune letterspacing or word spacing, to kern letters and even to distort letters can, in the hands of a skilled designer, produce optically correct text setting as the following examples show:

Correct letterspacing Cities were the cradle of civilis-ation. Was their original purpose defence, a negative response to pressure from outside? If so, no-one could have predicted that confining so many people in a restricted space would act as a nursery for social and individual creativity; but that seems to be	**Incorrect letterspacing** Cities were the cradle of civilisation. Was their original purpose defence, a negative response to pressure from outside? If so, no-one could have predicted that confining so many people in a restricted space would act as a nursery for social and individual creativity; but that seems to be what happened. The cities which housed

But kerning which has been well defined as 'the selective reduction of white space between irregularly shaped letters to create even optical spacing in a line of text copy' must be used with care. Wholesale kerning can produce ugly pairings of characters. Similarly distortion of letter forms – by type designers as well as by type users – must be limited and carefully thought out. As Matthew Carter explained at Type 90 'what makes distorted type unsatisfactory is that the whole letterform is either expanded or contracted by the same amount'. When type is condensed electronically, not only are the horizontal parts of the letter contracted, so too are the vertical stems, resulting in thinner vertical parts. Expanded type results in extra thick stems. Adrian Frutiger's comment that 'a small percentage of manipulation can give interesting results' is an appropriate summing-up.

Display type needs to be adjusted for optical correctness

Letter spacing and line spacing. In large display sizes it is important to adjust the letter spacing and the line spacing optically.

Another refinement which computer technology provides is the ability to align large initial letters – dropped or raised capitals – or large lowercase letters so that they fit optically with surrounding copy. Even with photocomposition it was never possible to obtain the detailed adjustments which certain letters require.

A STUDY OF THE editing stages can shed light on some of the main passages, but the date at which a particular passage was incorporated into the biblical text

THE CITIES had fallen. Even that would not, in former times, have meant the end of Sumer. What turned disaster into catastrophe now, what this time made it impossible for even

A STUDY OF THE editing stages can shed light on some of the main passages, but the date at which a particular passage was incorporated into the biblical text does not fix the date of

THE CITIES had fallen. Even that would not, in former times, have meant the end of Sumer. What turned disaster into catastrophe now, what this time made it impossible for even resilient

These large initial characters have been positioned to overlap the type measure so that they appear *optically* correct.

*f*or the fifth commandment guards the family. The last five commandments are, for their time, an astonishing enunciation of the moral basis of conduct. Astonishing, both because the principles are themselves new, but because for the very first time in history a god (or God) prescribes as law a specifically moral code. Gone are the days when law can express what wise judges have

A striking use of a large italic lowercase initial character.

With display setting it is even more important to introduce those detailed adjustments in word and line spacing, in 'letter-fitting' and in alignment which will produce optical correctness. Readers will be much more aware of unfortunate combinations of letters or words in large type sizes than they will in normal text setting.

The cost of fine-tuning

Refining computer-set material is, however, not inexpensive and introduces the additional question of how and at what stages the designer should implement his detailed control.

The first stage will be, as it was with hot metal and photo-composition, the provision of the detailed instructions for setting. If a typescript or hard-copy is available there is no problem, but if disks are supplied the temptation is there for the designer to become involved with the detailed keyboarding, which rarely makes commercial sense. Another contemporary problem is that so much of the keying is done by operators without the training which was essential in the older technologies. This means that designers inevitably require even more detailed knowledge of typographical style and art colleges will have to provide the necessary training.

Some of the problems that face designers were experienced in the production of this book. Because of the many contributors, all of whom are involved in technology, the texts for the various chapters were supplied on disk. Many different formats and programs were used by the individual authors and then had to be translated into a consistent Apple/QuarkXPress format. Not a nice job!

In fact some of the work done at this stage 'on computer' would have normally been done on paper at an earlier stage. For example, different conventions for bibliographical references were used by different authors. We tried to impose a uniform style, but this was rejected by some of the contributors (who corrected the proofs of their chapters back to the original.) The final outcome being an accommodation of diversity of styles along with unity of purpose.

Technology has resulted in important editorial decisions (which should be taken at an early stage) being left to the last minute and the traditional division of labour between editorial and design becoming blurred. This in some cases could be a disadvantage, resulting in books which may look good typographically but not editorially.

Bembo was chosen as the typeface because it has a classical, timeless feel and, with the expert font old style figures, true small capitals and extra ligatures were available. However, in Quark, where the expert font is found in the first line of text within a text box, the base line shifts down by about two points. This causes the text to overrun the bottom of the grid.

The second stage is to carry out the 'tweaking' on screen – in a way an extra and time-consuming stage – before the third stage, the detailed checking of a proof.

Developments will continue. What is essential is that designers ignore the technical gimmicks and concentrate on the new horizons offered by the new technology. To quote Aaron Burns, one of the Founders of the International Typeface Corporation;

> The problem that exists today is not the ability to produce fine typography, but the ability to recognise it when it is seen. To know what it should look like, what to try to achieve.

> Bad spacing is bad spacing in any era. If the tastefulness required to produce fine typography is not there, then fine typography will not be possible under any conditions using any technology.

PART *3*
MORE TECHNICAL ISSUES
INVOLVED IN TYPE DESIGN

Some aspects of the effect of technology on type design

MIKE DAINES DIRECTOR, SIGNUS LTD., SOUTH BANK TECHNOPARK,
LONDON SE1 6LN

'It is not necessary to carry out a more detailed examination of the technology in order to study the main ways in which the type designer interacts with digital type. In the short history of the relationship between type design and the computer, the issues have emerged fully, and the implications, for good or ill, are clear for us to see.'

Character description techniques in type manufacture

RICHARD SOUTHALL COMPUTER-TYPOGRAPHER AND RESEARCHER,
2 LONG ROW, WICKEN RD., LECKHAMPSTEAD, BUCKS. UK MK18 5NZ

A systematic view of type manufacturing systems is presented in which the emphasis is laid on the importance of communication of information about the appearance of character images within the system.

MIKE DAINES

Some aspects of the effects of technology on type design

The main factors which have influenced the development of letterforms – the writing instruments, the surfaces and the materials used for type – are clearly understood and have often been discussed. The advent of digital technology, however, blurred the hitherto well-defined parameters for the design and reproduction of type. It has also developed at such a pace that keeping track of the way in which type design and technology interact has become more complicated. Interestingly, the balance between the effect of technology on design, and way in which type design forces changes in that technology, continues to shift. This interplay is important because contemporary typefaces and typography are spreading their influences more widely through printed communication.

The first digital typesetters were recognized as the third generation of setting machines. Rudolf Hell demonstrated the first viable example, which used a cathode ray for imaging, in 1965. Laser technology completely opened up the field of non-photographic typesetting. The emergence of desktop publishing, using software which runs in personal computers and which links to personal typesetting devices, has dramatically widened the use of typefaces by professional and non-professional people alike. Digital type was potentially completely portable and accessible from the outset, and since 1985 there have been machine-independent type fonts.

Naturally enough, manufacturers of digital type first concerned themselves with overcoming the problems inherent in the task of reproducing existing typefaces in an authentic way. The drawbacks of digital imaging were immediately clear and 'low-resolution' soon became a synonym for 'low-quality' among designers, typographers, typesetters and printers. Just as the capacity of

Figure 1
Example of the
degradation of character
shape through lowering
of resolution on a crt
typesetter (as the size
decreases)

computer memory has increased in inverse proportion to cost, so digital resolution has increased, removing the 'jaggies' which characterize low-resolution digital typeforms. The next three years will see this process develop to the extent that 'bit-mapping' problems will cease to be an issue for printed output, and a considerably smaller problem for the screen representation of type.

The use of outline technology for the storage and handling of fonts also provides the appropriate technology for the better production and reproduction of type. Programs, particularly for the Apple Macintosh computer, have been written to allow the user to alter existing typefaces and to develop new ones for typesetting. This can be done for a fraction of the investment which has traditionally been needed for the manufacturing of type fonts, either in metal, for photocomposition, or for the creation of digital masters.

It is not necessary to carry out a more detailed examination of the technology in order to be able to study the main ways in which the type designer interacts with digital type. In the short history of the relationship between type design and the computer the issues have emerged fully, and the implications, good and bad, are clear for us to see.

There are three areas which are particularly important. First, the involvement of type designers with the early development of digital type and the approaches which were taken to solve the basic problems. Second, the evolution of software programs for the storage and, later, the design of digital type and their influences on new typefaces. Third, the way in which the accessibility of type design software has created the new 'type democracy', and the resulting effects on the standards of type design and typography.

All the major manufacturers of digital typesetting equipment recognized, as they entered the field, that they would need to involve type design specialists. This was particularly true of the traditional suppliers, such as Linotype and Monotype, who already had type production departments. Newer entrants, such as Autologic in California, USA, also saw that experience needed to be brought to bear on the detailed problems of the digital interpretation of letterforms as raster patterns.

As type designers working within manufacturing companies tackled the problems of digitally rendering typefaces, they gained invaluable experience which could later be applied to the design of new alphabets. At Autologic, for example, they included Summer Stone, who later ran the type department at Adobe and designed his own families of type.

The design of type for low resolution applications, such as dot-matrix printers and computer screens, is a specialist area which often uses typefaces bearing little relation to conventional printing types. There has been considerable experimentation in the simplification of letterforms, such as Wim Crouwel's designs from the 1960s. Crouwel presumed that type would mainly be displayed on VDUs in the future. His predictions seem less accurate now and such experimentation is largely regarded as redundant. At the same time, the design of special types for low to medium resolution printers (up to 300 lines per inch) has become an area of considerable progress. Charles Bigelow and Kris Homes cooperated to produce 'Lucida', a typeface family which was designed to overcome the limitations of such machines. Matthew Carter designed Charter, basing his letterforms on straight line segments, thus reducing the amount of data required and minimizing the problems encountered in the rasterizing of curves at low resolutions.

Fortunately the number of systems producers who rely on engineers to design type in the electronic publishing field is now very low, due partly to the competition from the 'typographic' laser printers and to the efforts of professional type designers who created early successes in the field.

At the upper end of digital resolution, in the area of typesetting, some new designs have emerged which have eased the passage to acceptability of the digital medium. The earliest examples were the designs produced by Hermann Zapf for the Hell company. Marconi, designed in 1976 for the Digiset machine, is the best known typeface in this series. Significantly, Marconi was the first typeface to be prepared for electronic typesetting using the Ikarus system.

Ikarus is a set of computer programs invented by Dr Peter Karow at URW in Hamburg in the early 1970s. At the heart of the programs is a unique method for storing the outlines of type characters using the descriptions of certain points around the contours of the letters and the precise locations of these points.

The programs proved important for type manufacturers who needed a standard method for storing type characters in a digital database. Having been established as the most satisfactory method for digitizing typefaces, the programs were developed further. The nature of their mathematics meant that it was relatively easy to create routines for the modifications of typefaces, including outlining, slanting, expanding, condensing and, most significantly, interpolating and extrapolating.

These last features, which provided the possibility for the computer-creation of additional weights for typefaces, gave type designers an easy route to extended type families. The typeface ranges of both manufacturers and type marketing companies like ITC, New York, soon showed evidence of dependence on

Figure 2
Example (from the Macintosh version of Ikarus) of the computer interpolation of a new character from bolder and lighter starting points.

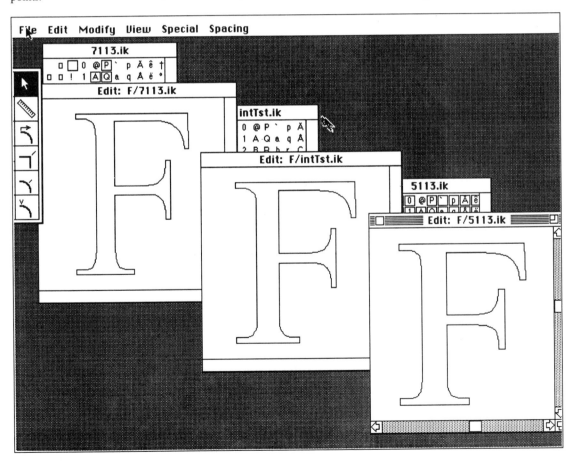

interpolation as a type design method. Like all computer-aided design programs, Ikarus depends for its successful use on skilled and critical operation. Used on this basis by designers like Zapf and Adrian Frutiger, it is an invaluable design tool. The uncritical use of modification programs, however, has swelled the number of digital types available from less discerning sources and has resulted in the curse of many unnecessary typeface weights.

The logical conclusion of the development of interpolation programs has been the creation of routines which allow for the mixing of the characteristics of typefaces from different families. This is a process which has become known as 'hybridization'. In this area the temptation for experimentation by less discerning designers has in some cases proved too great.

Otl Aicher's highly publicized typeface family, Rotis, completed in 1988, is unusual in that it includes sans serif, roman and intermediate variants, described as semi-sans serif and semi-roman. It seems unlikely that this project would have been undertaken before the existence of the Ikarus programs, and some of the letterforms show an over-dependence on the automatic results from the computer. It is a paradox that Aicher's stated objective for the Rotis family was optimum readability and yet the results of the hybridization process include some characters of unusual shape which hinder legibility.

Rapidly improving output resolution has made the task of preparing special typefaces for digital typesetting machines redundant and the lessons which have been learned about the effects of the laser and cathode ray on character reproduction can be left with technicians who are still concerned with lower-level devices.

Until the late 1980s type designers who wanted to work with computers needed access to systems which were installed only in type manufacturing centres. This restricted the use of the programs to experienced designers like Zapf and Aicher, who in turn were often working with design technologists who carried out the basic digitization and modification procedures. If the advent of desktop publishing was destined to put typography, typesetting and printing on the desktop, then why not type design and font production?

The Macintosh computer, the LaserWriter and Adobe Corporation's PostScript page description language are the three

Figure 3
Ikarus format, the
digitizing method
which has become an
industry standard.

most important elements of the dtp revolution. The PostScript
language uses the Bezier format for font and graphic outline
descriptions and it has already become the most widely used digital
format for type manipulation and typesetting. Ikarus remains
popular as a database format among manufacturers for storing
digital masters, but PostScript dominates for fonts for desktop
publishing and the Macintosh has become the most widely used
front-end system for typesetting.

The Macintosh, with its 'friendly' user interface, began to
encourage designers to make their own fonts almost from the
moment it arrived. The first typefaces produced in this way were
bitmaps, deliberately crude in appearance. The most famous are
those designed by Zuzanna Licko for her own Emigre magazine
which she published with Rudy Vander-Lans. These fonts are
intended to reflect the technology and in no way strive for
sophistication. Far more graphic designers, however, attempt to

LETRASET® CHARLOTTE™
began life as an experiment to see
if it was possible to design a traditional
typeface without any pencil drawings (or preliminary sketches) using Macintosh® technology
only. I chose LETRASET's *FontStudio®* as this was our
own product and I felt it was the most versatile Type
Design programme available for the Macintosh. This
involved constructing the characters on screen using
Bézier control points and keying in guide lines for cap
height, x-height, ascenders and descenders. Accents,
tabular & non-aligning numerals and a set of generic
characters were also designed. It was then spaced
and kerned. Although intending to design just
a book & a corresponding italic, I carried
on, producing **a medium, a bold**
AND A SET OF SMALL CAPS

Figure 4
Michael Gill's
'Charlotte', a typeface
created entirely at the
computer screen.

'improve' existing typefaces or design their own outline fonts using products such as Altsys Corporation's Fontographer program, Letraset's FontStudio or URW's Ikarus M. All these programs allow users to modify existing PostScript fonts and produce new designs 'on their own desktop'.

The fact that desktop type design and font production programs allow the user to create and manipulate character outlines means that it is not absolutely necessary to have the specialist knowledge gained by the producers of early digital 'bitmap' type. On the other hand, the outlines themselves are potentially more complex. Adobe's PostScript font format allows for the use of 'hints', elements in the character outline which define stems, curves and other parts, enabling their better reproduction at the printing stage. Apple's new format, 'TrueType', enables more hints to be added, leading to a sophisticated character outline which can be varied according to size and printing conditions.

ABCDEFGHIJKLM1234567890NOPQRSTUVWXYZ

CHARLOTTE Bold

¶This is Charlotte, a typeface designed totally on screen

CHARLOTTE Medium

USING FONTSTUDIO.‖A HIGH STANDARD OF EDITING, SPAC-

CHARLOTTE Book Italic

ing & kerning is obtainable, along with the ability to

CHARLOTTE Book

interpolate between weights.‖[§-2.41] Ranging and tabular

CHARLOTTE SMALL CAPS

(1.45−2.37) numerals.‖An old idea for new technology.

Much of this development means that the accurate production of a high quality PostScript font requires not just an understanding of type design principles but some technical knowledge. Whereas many of the technological answers can be found in the operating manuals, the typographic judgements required need a sounder knowledge base.

Through use of these programs a large number of new typefaces are appearing which are instantly accessible, although many are of poor typographic quality. The 'professional filters' have largely been removed. The typographer at the typesetting house who once would have excised errors of judgement is now by-passed as technology allows a complex piece of typography, typeset by the graphic designer on his Mac, perhaps using his own newly-created typeface, to go straight to the output device.

The new 'type democracy' brings with it a catalogue of potential advantages. Some skilled type designers need no longer be frustrated by years on the manufacturer's production waiting list before they can see their typefaces released. The development of 'custom', corporate and designs for special occasions is much more feasible, and valuable educational projects can be brought to market without the need for a wealthy sponsor.

The overall maintenance of typographic quality, however, presupposes considerably more education in type design and typography. Unfortunately, even a basic knowledge of the construction of letterforms, or calligraphy, cannot be assumed to be part of the contemporary graphic designer's toolkit. Major projects, including such important ones as the new typeface family for the Times newspaper, are created on Macintoshes far away from the drawing offices where years of experience were brought to bear in the creation of the original versions.

Should a new typeface be designed on screen, or using a pencil and paper in conjunction with a digitizing process? This, and other current debates, are rendered meaningless unless the designer wielding the pencil or the mouse has a basic knowledge of typeface construction.

Technology has the ability to free type design from artificial constraints. Without thorough education it also has the potential to create typographic chaos.

RICHARD SOUTHALL

Character description techniques in type manufacture

Introduction

In this chapter, four techniques for the definition of character shapes in type manufacture are examined and compared. Two of these are the traditional methods of punchcutting by hand and machine, used in the manufacture of metal type; the other two are bitmap font production and the production of mathematically specified contours of character shapes, used in the manufacture of digital type. The objective in making these comparisons is to consider alternatives which might exist to the contour-based font production methods that are almost universally used at the present day, and the characteristics that such alternatives might have.[1]

One motive for doing this is that there is a class of character design tasks for which contour-based design methods are quite unsuitable. These are the tasks which exploit to the limit the characteristics of particular character image production processes, in order to achieve the maximum possible legibility. Examples of such tasks are the design of fonts for telephone directory composition or for subtitling foreign-language material on broadcast television. The design of 'system' fonts for the display of text on computer visual display units ought to provide a third example; for a number of reasons, though, some of them technical and some not, it has failed to do so in the past [Bigelow85].

Another motive, allied to the previous one, is that there is an important character image specification task in which scaled and rasterized contours do not perform well, even with present-day scaling, hinting and rasterizing techniques. This is, of course, the automatic production of legible character images at sizes suitable for the display of text on computer visual displays, in which there

---

[1] Much of the argument presented here is developed from material which first appeared in a Stanford Computer Science Department report *Designing new typefaces with Metafont* [Southall85] and in a paper presented to the Protext III conference in 1986 [Southall86].

are fifteen pixels or fewer in the capital-letter height. Improving the performance of this particular task is considered in some quarters to be a low priority because the need for it arises from the relatively low resolutions of contemporary mark-making technologies, and these are always assumed to be on the point of substantial improvement. The fact is, though, that 72-dot-per-inch (dpi) displays and 300-dpi printers have been with us for almost a decade now, and show no sign of disappearing completely. It is from screens of 100-dpi resolution or less that the first generation of fully-developed hypertexts – informational material that cannot be studied otherwise than on computer displays – will be read.

A third motive for considering alternatives to contour-based character image specification methods is that there are some problems of character shape description for which contours seem to be inherently ill-suited. The whole of present-day contour-based font production technology was worked out in the first place with latin-script alphabets in mind. The contour that specifies the shape of a small *b* is reasonably simple in its configuration [Karow87, pp. 215–221] because the underlying structure of the character is simple; the same is true, more or less, of characters in other alphabetic and syllabic scripts. With ideographic scripts such as Kanji, though, most characters have structures of multiple intersecting strokes which are derived from patterns of overlapping brush-strokes (*cf.* [Moon&Shin90]). Contour descriptions of such characters are so complex, and the configurations of the contours relate so little to any intuitions about the structure of the characters themselves, that one wishes for a descriptive method that had more to do with the pattern of brush-strokes from which the character form is actually derived.

Punchcutting

The classic accounts of hand punchcutting are Moxon's of 1683 and Fournier's of 1766 [Moxon83; Fournier66]. Carter gives a useful summary [Carter69, ch. I]. The process still survives in a few hands [Drost85; Nelson86].

In the first stage of the process, the shape of the character to be produced is cut on the narrow end or *face* of a *punch*. The punch is a steel bar 5 or 6 cm in length and 5–10 mm square in cross-section for types intended for the composition of text.

The outer shape of the character is made by filing away the face of the punch at its edges. The inner shapes, or *counters*, of characters such as *B* or *e* are made by striking appropriately-shaped *counterpunches* into the face of the punch, or (for larger sizes and in later versions of the technique), with drills and gravers.

The punchcutter tests the progress of the work by making *smoke-proofs*. The face of the punch is blackened in a sooty flame and pressed on to a piece of smooth card; this yields a very clearly-defined reproduction of its shape.

When the punchcutter is satisfied with the appearance of the character, the punch is hardened by heat treatment. It is then struck into a block of copper to make a *matrix*. The matrix is *justified* by filing its face and its edges to ensure that it will produce type which has the correct width, alignment and height to paper, and is then used with a *mould* to cast type.

In hand punchcutting, the character shape on the face of the punch is made in its final size. An important consequence of working at final size, rather than by making large drawings and reducing them as happened in later techniques, is that the punchcutter does not have to take into account the effect that reduction in size has on the appearance of a shape. The shape on the end of the punch can be given its desired appearance directly. In working on the punch and making smoke-proofs, indeed, the punchcutter need not be explicitly concerned with the *shape* of the character at all; its shape is simply a vehicle for its appearance. Defects in the appearance of the image in the smoke-proof are corrected by modifying the shape on the punch, but in doing this the punchcutter does not need to be aware in any detail of the quantitative characteristics of the shape itself.

Mechanical punchcutting

Lynn Boyd Benton patented his pantographic punchcutting machine in 1885 (US patent 327855 of 1885). The machine was invented as an adjunct to another of Benton's inventions, 'self-spacing' type, in which the widths of all the characters and spaces were multiples of a basic unit, thus simplifying the compositor's task in justifying lines of text [Legros&Grant16, p. 77]. The production of such type, which had to be newly designed, called for quantities of new punches, and Benton developed his machine to provide them.

The starting-point for the pantographic cutting of a punch was a large drawing about 25 cm high on which the shape of a character was drawn as an outline [Legros&Grant16, p. 213; Gill36, ch. 3; Dwiggins40]. Metal patterns about 5 cm high were made from these drawings, also by pantographic reduction. At the punchcutting machine, an operator repeatedly traced around the contours of the pattern with 'followers' of progressively decreasing size, so that the path of the rotating cutter in the machine approximated more and more closely, though on a reduced scale, the outline of the pattern. Thus with Benton's machine it became possible for the first time to produce numbers of identical punches, and hence very large numbers of identical matrices.[2]

Benton's invention introduced to type manufacture the idea of the precisely-defined contour as a means of specifying character shape. This marked the end of type manufacture as a craft process and the beginning of its industrialization. Because Benton's machine required character shapes to be specified as contours, it demanded the production of drawings and hence brought about the separation between the activities of *designing* and *making* which is characteristic of industrial processes in general.

The manufacture of digital type

Digital photocomposition was introduced with the Digiset 50T1 machine in 1966 [Seybold84, ch. 9]. Because of speed limitations in the electronic hardware of the time, this machine, as well as almost all the high-speed cathode-ray-tube (CRT) composing machines that followed it, used bitmap fonts.

Bitmap font manufacture
These fonts were made for the most part by scanning on rotary-drum scanners the large character masters that were also used in matrix-making for direct-photography photocomposing machines, scaling the resulting very-high-resolution bitmaps with simple algorithms, and hand-editing on computer display terminals the 600–1000 dpi bitmaps which resulted. On CRT machines, each font could normally be scaled to produce output character images over

---

[2] Identical matrices could be produced from a single punch in the earlier technology. Sooner or later, though, the punch would break or wear out, and then it could not be replaced with one which was strictly identical.

a 2:1 or 3:1 range of sizes; on the laser imagesetters which followed them, each character image size required a separate font.

The scanning and scaling stages of this process were electronic analogues of the pattern-making and punchcutting stages of Benton's process, with the important difference that their numerical nature introduced errors the consequences of which had to be corrected at a later stage of the process. The necessity for manual intervention to make these corrections opened up the possibility that designers, rather than seeing their activities brought to an end with the production of the font producer's drawings, as had been the case with Benton's process, might work directly on the character shape specifications in the font.

This happened in two ways. In a few cases, where the legibility of the final product was paramount, designers made bitmaps directly [Mandel78; Cooper-Union82]. More frequently, details of the bitmaps produced by algorithmic scaling were modified to optimize the appearance of the output character images [Karow87, ch. 7]. Skilled designers could exploit the characteristics of particular marking processes to produce excellent results which were, however, completely device-specific [Rubinstein88, pp. 80-81].

Outline font manufacture
By the mid-1970s electronic processing power had become much cheaper than at the beginning of the decade, and it was possible to build photocomposing machines that interpreted character shape descriptions 'on the fly' into commands to a raster-scan CRT, rather than having to use previously prepared bitmaps. Early machines of this kind used shape descriptions made up of successions of straight-line vectors. These performed badly at large character image sizes, and were replaced at the beginning of the 1980s by arc-and-vector descriptions.

Machines of this type introduced the modern technology of font manufacture by contour digitization from large drawings [Flowers84; Karow87].

A systematic view of type manufacture

We can think of a *type manufacturing system* as a system that incorporates the whole set of operations involved in developing new designs for typefaces and producing the fonts that realize them.

Typefaces and fonts

Typefaces are sets of appearance specifications for the characters of a script. They are produced by a *type designer.*

Fonts are components of a document production system, in which their function is to specify the configurations of character images to the *marking device* which is also part of the system. Fonts are manufactured objects, produced on an industrial scale. As with all such objects, special knowledge and skills are involved in their production. We can describe as *font producers* the people who possess such knowledge and exercise such skills.

A single typeface can be realized by numbers of different fonts produced by several different manufacturers.

In a type manufacturing system, the task of the type designer is to prepare sets of character appearance specifications in a form in which they are useful to a font producer. The task of the font producer is to make objects which, when the specifications in them are interpreted by a marking device, will give rise to character images whose appearance corresponds to the specifications prepared by the type designer.

Models and pattern

The issue of communication between type designer and font producer is of central importance in a type manufacturing system. If the appearance characteristics of the typeface are to be realized in the character images which result from the font producer's work, the producer must be able to learn from the designer what those characteristics are. Equally, the designer must be able to discover from the producer the extent to which the appearance of the character images yielded by a font under development corresponds to the specifications in the typeface the font is intended to realize.

Because appearance is a visual matter, the commonest and most effective mode of communication between designer and producer in traditional technologies of type production has been a graphic one. In this mode, the designer makes drawings of character shapes and shows them to the font producer, and the font producer makes proofs of type and shows them to the designer.

It is important to understand the role that the designer's drawings play in graphic-mode dialogues of this kind. They serve almost invariably as *models*: objects whose purpose is to illustrate the desired appearance of the typeface to the producer.

In mechanical punchcutting and the manufacturing technologies that have followed it, the font producer also makes drawings. These have a subject-matter which is different from that of the designer's drawings. The font producer's drawings are about *shape*, not appearance; their purpose is specify the shapes of other intermediates in the font production process. Drawings of this kind are *patterns*: objects which contain precise specifications for the shapes of other objects.

Developing the font
In metal–type manufacture, font development proceeds by iterative modification and testing of the character shapes on the punches. Matrices are struck from the punches and justified, type is cast from them and proofed, and the appearance of the character images in the proof is assessed to find the extent to which it corresponds with the appearance specifications in the original design.

Because the character images in the proof are small, corrections to them are necessarily concerned with their appearance rather than their shape. This presents no difficulty to the hand punchcutter, who corrects the appearance of the smoke-proofs directly by modifying and testing the shapes on the punches. With pantographic punchcutting, the problem is not so simple. The font producer has to convert the designer's quantitative remarks about the appearance of character images into precise quantitative modifications to the shapes on the pattern drawings.

With contour font manufacture, the problem is more complicated still. The configuration of the character images in the proof, and hence their appearance, is a threefold consequence of the shapes specified by the contours, the characteristics of the rasterizing algorithm which interprets the contours into the patterns of dots and lines specified to the marking engine, and the marking process by which the dots and lines are made visible. In deciding how to convert a correction to the appearance of a character image into a modification to the shape of the character's contour, the font producer has to be able to disentangle all of these factors from one another.

The notion of the glyph

In metal-type manufacture, the sub-processes which followed the production of punches in the manufacturing process had effects of their own on the eventual shapes of the characters on the types. Striking the punch into the soft copper of the matrix, for example, would tend to round out the interior angles of acute-angled junctions between strokes. Unlike the effects of the marking process, the exact extent of such effects could be anticipated with experience, and the character shapes on the punches modified to compensate for them. The effects themselves, though, were inherent in the manufacturing process and could not be circumvented.

In present-day technology, in just the same way, the interpretation by the rasterizing algorithm of the character shape specification in a contour font, which is essential to the production of character images, has its own effects on the configuration of the images which are eventually produced. Because the rasterizing algorithm is deterministic, its effects can be completely predicted; but, equally, they cannot be interactively modified at the time of production of the character images if these turn out to be unsatisfactory.

Hence there is a point, in both traditional and present-day type manufacture, beyond which neither designer nor producer can interact with the font production process to achieve a particular set of graphic objectives in the character images the font will eventually produce. Human intervention becomes impossible, and the impersonal and unalterable characteristics of the technology itself take over. We can refer to the character shape specifications that exist at this point in the font production process as *glyphs*.[3]

In hand punchcutting, the glyphs are the completed punches; in

[3] This use of *glyph* differs from Rubinstein's. He uses the term to denote the concept for which I use *character image*: 'The individual symbols in a font are called glyphs when they are printed' [Rubinstein88, p. 16].

Benton's process, they are the patterns from which the punch is cut; and in contour font manufacture they are the character shape descriptions which are sent to the rasterizer.

A quality criterion for type manufacturing systems
For salespeople, accountants and systems engineers, a good type manufacturing system is *useful*: it should be possible to use its products with as many type-composing machines as possible. From this point of view, contour digitization is a winner. Like Benton's machine, it produces intermediates which can be used to make fonts for many – if not all – of the document production systems of its epoch.

There is another group, though, who are also entitled to make demands of a type manufacturing system. These are the designers whose work provides the input to the system, and, in a sense, the justification for its existence. For a designer, a good type manufacturing system is above all *responsive*. A responsive system allows the designer to make any technically practicable mark; it does not intrude itself between the designer and the development of a graphic idea, nor does it impose too long a delay on the idea's realization as a character image.

From this point of view, type manufacturing systems incorporating pantographic punchcutting did not perform at all well. Several significant features emerge from contemporary designers' accounts of their work with industrialized type manufacturing organizations [Gill36; Dwiggins40; vanKrimpen57,72; Zapf60]. The first is how much less direct the process of developing character shapes was in the industrial technique than in hand punchcutting. The designer would make a design and give it to the font producer. Some time later, a proof of the type would appear; the designer would mark corrections on the proof and return it, and some time later still a corrected proof would come back. This long interval between specifying a modification to a shape and seeing its results is not surprising, given the complexity of the manufacturing process, but it contrasts very unfavourably with the immediacy of punch and smoke-proof.

The second striking feature of contemporary accounts is the difficulty that even experienced designers had in anticipating the appearance of character shapes which had been drawn large when they were seen small. '*Curves* do all kinds of queer things when reduced; and the way lines running together make spots is a thing that will surprise you ' [Dwiggins40].

The third feature, on which all the designers are unanimous, is the problem of ensuring that the manufacturing process did not impose an undesirable degree of uniformity on their designs. 'It is now a dogged tussle over form, the designer on one side armed only with pencil and pen, and on the other his numerically superior opponents, fully mechanized and equipped with machines of utmost refinement. Woe, if the machine wins out and the characters are shaped after its judgement! Who will then need to wonder if the emergent letter is cold and soulless?' [Zapf60].[4]

In their comments about industrial type manufacture, the designers often harked back to the directness and immediacy of hand punchcutting. Generalizing from this, as well as from more recent comments and experience (*cf.* [Mandel78, Zapf85]), we can suggest that, in the terms of the present discussion, type manufacturing systems improve from the designer's point of view as the moment at which the glyph is defined comes later and later in the process of making the font. Alternatively, a manufacturing system will remain acceptable to designers if the processes that follow the definition of the glyph have little or no effect on the character image configuration specified in the glyph.

Alternatives to contour digitization

The challenge in designing a type manufacturing system – to the extent that such a thing is ever done explicitly – is to combine in it to the greatest extent possible the qualities of responsiveness and usefulness. We can see what this might mean by considering two possible alternatives to contour digitization as manufacturing techniques. These are bitmap editing, and techniques for specifying character shapes by means of programs.

Bitmap editing

Bitmap editing methods score highly on responsiveness, even with the primitive implementations that have been available to designers in the past (*cf.* [Cooper-Union82], in which one page shows a run-

---

[4] It is fair to add that the period also saw some more congenial collaborations: *cf.* [Tracy86, ch. 16].

length-encoded character shape specification written out in the designer's handwriting). This is because the technique, like hand punchcutting, gives the designer the maximum possible control over the behaviour of the marking device. It is impossible to overlook the commercial disadvantages of a manufacturing technique which can only produce device-specific bitmaps; equally, though, it is impossible to ignore the attractiveness to designers of a technique in which the definition of the glyphs comes right at the end of the manufacturing process.

Shape-specification techniques
The most fully documented example of this approach is Metafont [Knuth86]. More recent work in this area has used PostScript, which has the advantage over Metafont in that a program specifying the shape of a character can capture information about the graphic context in which a character image finds itself at the moment of its production [André&Borghi89, André&Delorme90].

Although my own comments on Metafont have been unfavourable in the past (*cf.* [Southall85]), I now believe that two of the ideas incorporated in it point to directions which might be profitable for future research.

Metafont can specify any technically practicable mark, but its scores on the other criteria for responsiveness are so poor that it is effectively unusable as a manufacturing system. However, it scores very highly indeed on usefulness. The troublesome problems of low-resolution rasterization and non–linear scaling of character shapes are completely solved in Metafont. This is because the language effectively allows its users to tell a target marking device how to construct a character shape, rather than presenting the device with an ideal shape and telling it to approximate it as best it can.

The other powerful idea, which unlike the idea of giving instructions to the marking device is latent rather than overt in Metafont, results from Knuth's wish to incorporate 'the "intelligence" that lies behind a design' in the programs which describe the design [Knuth85]. The declarative nature of the Metafont language goes some way to achieving this objective, in allowing desired relationships between the elements of character shapes to be specified directly. However, the only means available at present for the designer/programmer to say why the relationships are specified in one way rather than another is by adding comments to the program.

An appearance-based approach to the design of type design systems
We have already seen that appearance is the subject-matter of the type designer's work, and of the dialogue between designer and font producer. Designers manipulating bitmaps, like designers cutting punches, are trying to achieve particular appearance characteristics in the images they produce. If we contemplate the design of a type manufacturing system from this point of view, the question irresistibly presents itself, 'Is it possible to make a computer-based system which deals with appearance directly, but in a device-independent way?'

The first task in implementing such a system would be to develop techniques which allowed the appearance of character images to be described in absolute terms. In dialogues between designers and font producers in which the appearance of character images is discussed, the designers' comments are couched in comparative terms: '*diese Partie ist zu leicht*' (this part is too light); '*evt. etwas breiter*' (perhaps somewhat wider) when they are not less explicit still: '*Bogen schlecht*' (curve bad).[5] Remarks of this kind refer to understandings about the appearance of character images which are shared between designer and font producer but which are not, and in the context of a dialogue between skilled practitioners do not need to be, spelt out by either side.

A possible approach to the problem of providing an absolute description of the appearance of a character image is to describe its shape, and then to relate its shape to its appearance in some precise but general way. This approach presents a number of difficulties. For one thing, if we think of shapes as being defined by mathematically tractable contours, it may not be at all clear what shape the image has whose appearance we are trying to describe. Low-resolution bitmaps do not have shapes in this sense; nor do the character images in early printed books. It may be possible to ascribe contour-defined shapes to the latter, but such ascriptions always involve a substantial element of interpretation [Dreyfus66].

5 These are some of Zapf's corrections to a proof of 36 pt Optima foundry type [Zapf87, p. 195].

Another difficulty emerges when we try to establish the general relationships between the shapes of images and their appearance which are called for by this approach. Karow illustrates and presents data on the well-known discrepancy between the appearance characteristic of *size* and the shape characteristic of *calibre* [Karow87, ch. 2 and Appendix E]. Ryder illustrates a similar discrepancy between the *slope* and *slant* of character strokes [Ryder79, pp. 76–77]. I have already mentioned the difficulty of assessing the appearance of large shapes when they are reduced. We do not have theoretical explanations for any of these effects, nor can we generalize from Karow's data, even to shapes which differ only in their ratio of stroke thickness to calibre.[6]

My own sense of the problem is that trying to find a theory of the relationships between contour-defined shapes and their appearance is not a useful exercise, and that methods of characterizing appearance which have to do with the amount and disposition of colour in a character image have a greater chance of success. (*Colour* is used here in the typographer's sense, referring to the marking material which makes the image visible.) From this point of view, it is the configuration of the image which is important for its appearance; the shape of its contour, if it has one at all, is secondary.

Elements of the image interact visually with one another and with the elements of adjacent images in ways which type designers and typographers understand, even if they cannot speak about them in explicit terms, and which in principle are susceptible of mathematical analysis [John Lane, personal communication]. (Kindersley and Wiseman's work on computing intercharacter spacing seems to me to be an alternative realization of the same idea, although it is not concerned with images of limited resolution [Kindersley&Wiseman79].)

Thus the key to an understanding of the problems of low-resolution rasterization and non-linear scaling of character shapes is to be found not in the mathematics of polynomial curves but in the characteristics of the human visual system. Work on feature detection in early vision – the 'pre-attentive' phase of visual perception – seems so far to have concentrated on the mechanisms

---

[6] Perception of the size of a hollow triangle of a given external calibre is strongly influenced by the calibre of the internal shape.

by which information about the three-dimensional external world is extracted from the grey-scale array on the retina [Marr82]. It seems possible, at least, that the same psychological and neurobiological data, considered from a different perspective, might yield explanations of the visual effects which occur in the perception of two-dimensional character images. Such explanations, like the theories of visual perception on which they are based, would be computational. If they could be found, they would open up the possibility of building computer-based type design systems which, like punchcutters and the producers of bitmap fonts, deal directly with the appearance of the images they produce.

Acknowledgement

This paper was first published in Raster Imaging and Digital Typography II 1991, editors; Morris RA and Andrè J, it is reproduced here by kind permission of Cambridge University Press.

References

[André&Borghi89] Jacques André & Bruno Borghi, "Dynamic Fonts", in J. André & R. D. Hersch (eds.), *Raster imaging and digital typography*, Cambridge University Press, 1989, pp. 198–204.

[André&Delorme90] Jacques André & Christian Delorme, "Le Delorme, un caractère modulaire et dépendant du contexte", *Communications et langages*, no. 86, 1990, pp. 65–76.

[Bigelow85] Charles Bigelow, "Font design for personal workstations", *Byte*, vol. 10 no. 1, January 1985, pp. 255–270.

[Carter69] Harry Carter, *A view of early typography*. Oxford: Clarendon Press, 1969.

[CooperUnion82] *Matthew Carter: Bell Centennial*, Type & technology monograph no. 1. New York: Cooper Union, 1982.

[Drost85] Henk Drost, "Punchcutting demonstration", *Visible language*, vol. 19 no. 1, 1985, pp. 99–105.

[**Dreyfus**66] John Dreyfus, *Italic quartet*. Cambridge: Cambridge University Press (privately printed), 1966.

[**Dwiggins**40] W. A. Dwiggins, *WAD to RR: a letter about designing type*. Cambridge, Mass.: Harvard College Library, 1940.

[**Flowers**84] Jim Flowers, "Digital type manufacture: an interactive approach", *IEEE Computer*, May 1984, pp. 40–48.

[**Fournier**66] Simon-Pierre Fournier, *Manuel typographique*. Paris: Fournier, 1764 (vol. I), 1766 (vol. II).

[**Gill**36] Eric Gill, *An essay on typography*. London: Sheed & Ward, 1936.

[**Karow**87] Peter Karow, *Digital formats for typefaces*. Hamburg: URW Verlag, 1987.

[**Kindersley&Wiseman**] David Kindersley & Neil Wiseman, "Computer aided letter design', *Printing world*, 31 October 1979, pp. 12–13, 17.

[**Knuth**85] Donald E. Knuth, "Lessons learned from Metafont", *Visible language*, vol. 19 no. 1, 1985, pp. 35–53.

[**Knuth**86] Donald E. Knuth, *The Metafontbook*. Reading, Mass.: Addison-Wesley, 1986.

[**Legros&Grant**16] Lucien Alphonse Legros and John Cameron Grant, *Typographical printing-surfaces*. London: Longmans, Green & Co., 1916.

[**Mandel**78] Ladislas Mandel, "Il nuovo carattere Galfra per gli elenchi telefonici italiani", *Graphicus*, vol. 9, 1978.

[**Marr**82] David Marr, *Vision*. New York: Freeman, 1982.

[**Moon&Shin**90] Y. S. Moon & T. Y. Shin, "Chinese fonts and their digitization", in R. Furuta (ed.), *EP90*, Cambridge University Press, 1990, pp. 235–248.

[**Moxon**83] Joseph Moxon, *Mechanick exercises on the whole art of printing* (1683). Edited by H. Davis and H. Carter (2nd edition). Oxford: Oxford University Press, 1962; New York: Dover, 1978.

[Nelson86] Stan Nelson, "Cutting Anglo-Saxon sorts", in C. Bigelow, P. H. Duensing & L. Gentry (eds.), *Fine Print on type*, Lund Humphries, 1989.

[Rubinstein88] Richard Rubinstein, *Digital typography – an introduction to type and composition for computer system design*. Reading, Mass.: Addison-Wesley, 1988.

[Ryder79] John Ryder, *The case for legibility*. London: The Bodley Head, 1979.

[Seybold84] J. W. Seybold, *The world of digital typesetting*. Media, Pa.: Seybold, 1984.

[Southall85] Richard Southall, *Designing new typefaces with Metafont*. Computer Science Department Technical Report STAN-CS-85-1074, Stanford University, California, 1985.

[Southall86] R. Southall, "Shape and appearance in typeface design", in J. J. H. Miller (ed.), *Protext III: proceedings of the third international conference on text processing systems*, Boole, 1986, pp. 75–86.

[Tracy86] Walter Tracy, *Letters of credit: a view of type design*. London: Gordon Fraser, 1986.

[vanKrimpen57] Jan van Krimpen, *On designing and devising type*. New York: The Typophiles, 1957.

[vanKrimpen72] Jan van Krimpen, *A letter to Philip Hofer on certain problems connected with the mechanical cutting of punches*. Cambridge, Mass.: Harvard College Library, 1972.

[Zapf60] Hermann Zapf, *About alphabets: some marginal notes on type design*. New York: The Typophiles, 1960.

[Zapf85] Hermann Zapf, "Future tendencies in type design", *Visible language*, vol. 19 no. 1, 1985, pp. 23–33.

[Zapf87] Hermann Zapf, *Hermann Zapf & his design philosophy*. Chicago: Society of Typographic Arts, 1987.

PART 4
LESSONS TO BE LEARNED FROM THE HISTORY OF TYPOGRAPHY

Education in the making and shaping of written words

FERNAND BAUDIN BOOK DESIGNER AND TYPOPHILE, 39, CHEMIN DE L'HERBE, BONLEZ, 1325 BELGIUM

No method ever affected our general education as deeply as typography once did or as the computer is doing currently. The nearest PC has at least one lesson for you: without a memory it is useless. We are witnessing what happened within a mere seventy years after a deliberate attempt to cut off the past. The important thing is to share with the masters the criteria by which any piece of work can be rated – and respected where respect is due.

A typographer by any other name

ALAN MARSHALL ARCHIVIST, MUSEUM OF PRINTING, 13 RUE DE LA POUAILLERIE, 69002 LYON FRANCE

Have the new personal computer based techniques fundamentally diminished the role of the typographical specialist as their promoters once claimed they would? Has the printed word irremediably suffered at the hands of the computer engineers as typographical purists once feared?... Each new machine takes automation a step further, but the pool of typographical knowledge is not limited. It too is constantly expanding. Each new tool increases the typographer's power – assuming that the typographer knows how to use it and to what end.

FERNAND BAUDIN

Education in the making and shaping of written words

The truth is that education is one of those rather delusive words which decoy us into talking public nonsense, to our own bewilderment and to the bewilderment of those who hear us ... Therefore, personally I never talk about education if I can avoid it, but I am always ready to talk about children and teachers and schools and staffing. Those are facts, which you cannot get over.

Thus spoke George Sampson (1878-1950) on 8 February 1944, as reported in Whitehouse (1945), at a luncheon held to commemorate the birth of John Ruskin. As an Inspector of Schools, he wanted less of the Three R's and more of the Three Graces. As a matter of fact, we have today much less of the Three R's (at least so we are told by the media) and we are overwhelmed by a chronic deluge of playmates where Sampson was content with a mere Three Graces. As Sampson said in 1944, 'Education is very much in the air today'. So it is now as it was in the days of Henry Adams, Locke, Augustinus or Plato. And the overall situation today is as chaotic as it may have been in any city state or empire in the remotest past right back to Sumer.

I have never been an Inspector of Schools but, because of the combination of my life as a professional book designer and my research in a field described by another delusive word 'Writing' (109 lines and 19 cross references in Roget's Thesaurus) I would like to offer a new point of view on a very wide perspective.

Education in literacy, wherever it exists, is reportedly in a quandary for any number of reasons which I do not profess to know. At least, not all of them. One of them is admittedly the computer. This method of 'printing' has indeed overthrown all the professional compartments and partitions which gave a sense of order and security to all the people involved. They felt secure because they thought they knew what they were doing whenever they were using their particular and familiar tools. In fact, except for the invention of writing itself and Gutenberg's invention of the adjustable mould, the case, the chase and the printing press, no method better revealed the perennial chaos to be overcome by education than the change involving the computer. (We must not forget, however, that the Chinese invented movable type centuries earlier than Gutenberg.) Like other professional tools, several typographic tools have been replaced by others. Yet, in this case, we feel we have lost more than our tools. We have lost our bearings, as well as our sense of direction. Now we feel that our traditional education is no longer a link with our past or an answer for the present. No one really knows what is to come. A sense of chaos has replaced our sense of direction. Yet . . .

The horse-drawn car has been superseded by the motor car. The motor car has also completely altered our daily environment and our lifestyle. Not to mention the telegraph, the telephone and the 'flying machine'. But no machine has ever affected our education as deeply as the typographic method once did, or the computer is doing today. I suspect that this is the reason why most people, not least the media, are in the position of apprentice sorcerers and turn to education in the abstract, while the rest — the live educators themselves — do not seem to know any more or any better than the next reporter, inspector or whatever. Do I? Of course not, but I would like to make a contribution under the heading 'Education in Making and Shaping the Written Word', as distinct from 'Writing, Calligraphy, Typewriting and Typography' as they have been taught ever since education became compulsory. Ever since commercial and administrative transactions began to be typed instead of handwritten, ever since longhand was considered expendable as a menial task, unworthy of 'the elite' (expressions translated from Mialaret and Vial 1981) and soon to be replaced by the telephone or some other invention of this 'wonderfully inventive age' as Edgar Alan Poe called it.

First let me introduce myself by presenting my credentials as a professional book designer who has been dealing with abstractions as well as facts — if only because all the former 'handy work' of letter making and shaping are becoming daily more abstract.

After graduating from an art school founded in Brussels by

Henry Van de Velde (1863-1957), I have been working and making a living as a book designer. As such, I have also been watching what I myself and all the people around me have been doing. Wherever I have gone and worked, as a freelance or as a captive designer, I have had to deal with publishers and printers. All of us have been very busy using ready-made typefaces in the making up of books, magazines, ads and daily newspapers. We have all taken the whole process for granted, even when hot-metal and the printing press were replaced by photocomposition and offset. This may well account for a growing sense of disbelief I have had ever since I instinctively started my research by dipping into Edward Johnston's *Writing and Illuminating and Lettering* (1906). Never intending to become a calligrapher, I was only trying to understand what these ready-made letterforms had to do with my own handwriting and with all the printed matter with which I was dealing; books, weeklies, dailies, monthlies, ads, etc.

I was granted a degree after more or less two years in the Atelier d'Ornementation du Livre (as distinct from illustration) and later, in the fifties, was accepted as a designer for the catalogues of the Royal Library at Brussels. There I had direct access to manuscripts and rare books. I was therefore able, gratefully, to study the real things, not just their reproductions. It was also where and when I started to ask myself questions about education as it was. For I soon discovered that even learned people, some of them pioneers in the field now known as codicology, would analyze every stroke of a medieval pen, but would consult me rather than let themselves be involved in typography – which, to me, seemed a much easier task, a mere matter of taste, as against their hard work. Needless to say, taste seemed and still seems to me to be just as important as hard work. Where taste is lacking, a mess is the result. And more so the harder you work.

The ordinary literate people paid no attention whatsoever to all the letterforms which made up – and still do – their environment and which they were daily using professionally and otherwise, if only as readers. They thought they had and knew all that was needed. They were quite content with their handwriting as it was. Anything else was someone else's business, profession or whatever. They could not be bothered, except when they had to foot the bill. Then, when they asked questions, the answers had nothing to do with printing types, their use and history. To them it was always a surprise whenever they heard about serifs, thicks and thins, ascenders, descenders, etc., and they were even more convinced that this was none of their business.

In the sixties, by the time that hot metal was replaced by cold type and a new era was heralded by Marshall McLuhan, I was working as a layout man with Typefoundry Amsterdam and G.W. Ovink. Ovink introduced me to John Dreyfus, who persuaded himself and Stanley Morison to let me organize the first ever exhibition on *Stanley Morison et la tradition typographique* (1966). This led me to Lurs-en-Provence, where I met Maximilian Vox and the international community of typographers. It was Vox who encouraged Rémy Magermans, John Dreyfus and myself to collect and print privately the results of our enquiries into the *mise en page* and the teaching of handwriting and lettering.

By the time the computer was in the offing, Vox was no longer around and John Dreyfus invited me to join the Association Typographique Internationale (ATypI), Charles Peignet and most of the better type designers of this century. So much about myself, my sources and my professional environment.

This perhaps is not the place for a lengthy discourse on the history and developments within ATypI and the École de Lure. Suffice it to say that soon the interests divided into those concerned exclusively with cultural matters, e.g. an international *classification* of typefaces, and others who were exclusively concerned with the international *protection* of typefaces. Few people within ATypI or Lure thought that handwriting had anything to do with type design or type protection (except, of course, Nicolete Gray, Michael Twyman, the first chairman of the Committee of Educators, Gerrit Noortzij and, later, Rosemary Sassoon).

Incidentally, while the successors of those involved in the "Rencontres Internationales de Lure" fulfilled the hopes of Vox, namely drawing official attention to the subject of typography, ATypI never achieved its declared goal concerning type protection.

At Vienna on 12 June 1973, the text of an *Agreement for the Protection of Typefaces and their International Deposit* was approved by the World International Property Organization (WIPO). However, a minimum of five States had to ratify this Agreement to constitute what WIPO calls a Union for the Protection of Typefaces. By the end of 1991 only France and Germany had ratified it.

On 15 October 1974, Hermann Zapf, as the leading calligrapher-typographer in the world, was given the opportunity to address the members of the Copyright Office at the Library of Congress, Washington D.C. in order to try and convert them to the idea of protecting the intellectual and industrial rights of type design and type manufacturing. He failed. This is no reason to give up the idea of type protection, an idea which is almost as old as punchcutting. On the contrary, this is one more relevant reason to do some solid thinking and to reconsider all that is involved in 'typography' as distinct from what I choose to describe as 'making and shaping written words' (using Sampson's phrase). Hermann Zapf drew his own conclusions years ago in 1983, in Stanford, when he said, 'In alphabet design – I do not want to use the word type design any more, for type design to me means metal, and is associated with Gutenberg's invention for casting type – we should take advantage of today's possibilities and needs, using the new tools like Ikarus and Metafont.' Thus he made a clearcut distinction between the design of alphabets and the method of producing them.

Things were beginning to move in the outside world by then, but whatever initiatives were being carried out locally, officialdom was not yet prepared to include calligraphy and/or typography in the curriculum of non-professional schools. Then, on 20 December 1976, President Valéry Giscard d'Estaing asked his Inspecteur Général des Finances, Simon Nora, to report on what should be done in order to harness the computer in the service of a democratic community. A report was duly delivered and, among other things, stated that the present generation is undergoing a mutation second only to the invention of writing. This report was closely followed, on 13 February 1984, by the letter that President Mitterand addressed to the Administrateur of the Collège de France which asked his colleagues how they would formulate the first principles for an education system in which 'the most universal literary and artistic culture would be integrated with the most recent achievements made by the most recent scientific methods'. The answer was duly published by the Collège de France. One passage in particular reassured me. Regarding a 'minimum culturel commun' it said: 'Here again the dismissal of hierarchies should lead, *especially at the primary level* (my italics) to teach, next to the fine arts, the applied arts so useful in our daily life, such as graphic arts, publishing arts and publicity . . .'

I had long been advocating 'Education' within ATypI when F. Richaudeau in 1984, asked me to write something about handwriting. This I did in longhand under the title 'Typography how it works, why it is important' showing how typography should and could be taught in the classroom on the blackboard. Why typography when handwriting was in fact the real assignment? Because all I know about the teaching of handwriting is that I have been wondering for 42 years how to relate typography to handwriting. Subsequently I did more research which brought some new results. Although I thought I had no more to say, I found that I did. The following, then, is a preview of what is to be published this year as *L'Effet Gutenberg*.

The inventions of Gutenberg had countless effects. It would take any number of experts just to list all the works of the scholars who have explored the subject. They are totally unknown to the public and I list just two, Eisenstein (1970) and Hellinga (1989). While most people have heard about McLuhan's 'The Gutenberg Galaxy' (The media took care of that because he was a very talented prophet of doom.) Yet he did not contribute anything to help the people concerned with the future of literacy. On the contrary, it can be argued that his oracular pronouncements have led quite a number of people into believing that they are individually doomed in what they consider to be their gutenbergian activities, whatever that means to them.

My concern was with the impact that Gutenberg's inventions had on education in literacy. However, that was not my starting point. As I said earlier, my starting point was the growing contempt of the educators for handwriting, which resulted from the simultaneous introduction of the typewriter, the composing machines and compulsory education a century ago. This contempt is now culminating, at least in some quarters, in a total dismissal of handwriting as a relevant means of communication and in a sanguine confidence that the computer and virtual reality will soon be adequate substitutes for any true reality. This has been ridiculed by, amongst others, Edgar Allan Poe in English and Villiers de l'Isle

Adam in French. In vain. *Le ridicule ne tue plus.* Some mistakes do. In education mistakes are economic disasters as well as soul destroying.

This contempt was not the beginning of a new era but the end of a long process of fragmentation which I call 'the Gutenberg Effect' because I have come to the conclusion that it started with Gutenberg's inventions. How is that? Because they disrupted the age-old Western methods for making and shaping written words by hand. How? By bodily separating those who make the letterforms from those who shape them into a text as printed matter.

Until that time anyone who was educated at all knew right from the beginning that education was all about learning how to read and how to write – regardless of the subject. And that whole process culminated in a university where one was expected to achieve a mastery over articulate speech in the practice of disputation, and a mastery over articulate handwriting in the making of books. Not necessarily as a calligrapher, but as such a one, who by his own Judgement, from solid reasoning with himself, can either perform, or direct others to perform from the beginning to the end all the Handyworks and physical Operations relating to the making and the shaping of the most elaborate and articulate piece of writing known as a book, i.e. any number of quires between two covers and a binding.

The best evidence of this can be found not only in the fifteenth century manuscripts and in the earliest printed books, but also in the ballads of François Villon, who may, incidentally, have met Peter Schöffer at the Sorbonne, where both were students in 1449. Peter Schöffer made a living as a calligrapher and manuscript copyist. Later he became an associate of Gutenberg and the son-in-law of Johann Fust in Mainz. François Villon was a master of arts, a thief, a murderer, and a pimp, even as he was winning immortality as a French poet. Fremin, a fellow student is only remembered as an amanuensis who could take down Villon's dictation, who knew what to do next, and where to go in order to have any number of copies made 'everywhere'. In French '*Puis faict le partout coppier*' (From *Le Testament Villon*, LXXIX). This last verse is an embarrassment to even the more specialized Villonists, just as plano manuscripts have been to icunabulists and codicologists since 1958. This is a good example of what I mean by 'the Gutenberg Effect'.

We have no description of his invention by Gutenberg himself. But Johann Fust, who was his sponsor, and Peter Schöffer, who was an associate of both, wrote the earliest description in the colophon of the famous *Psalter* (printed in Mainz in 1457). They say, in Latin, '*Adinventione artificiosa imprimendi ac caracterizandi absque calami ulla exaracione*' – that their psalter was produced by means of an invention allowing them to print artfully '*and to write without a pen*' (my italics). In England, Caxton, in the epilogue to the third and last part of his *Recuyell* (1471), insists that 'it is not wreton with penne and ynke, as other books ben'. Giambattista Palatino in his *Libro Nelqual s'Insigna a Scriver* (Rome, 1545) describes printing '*alla Stampa, ch'altro non e, che un scriver senza penna*'. Christophe Plantin, in his *Dialogues François* (1597), speaks of '*écrire à la presse sans plume*'. The description was used so frequently that when Greek had been revived long enough, and had become fashionable enough, a new Greek word, 'typography', was coined in order to describe a method by which 'calligraphy' could be *written without a pen*. As a result, to this day, no one except 'calligraphers' or readers of Edward Johnston have any idea of what was implied as an essential part of 'calligraphy' i.e., 50% of the *ars artificialiter scribendi*, namely, pricking and ruling. This procedure is essential – practically, visually – and financially. Practically and visually wherever order is desirable for the sake of perspicuity; financially, because otherwise there is no way to calculate how much space, time and material will go into the copying of a given number of letters in a chosen size and in a book format of the intended dimensions. Or needless to say, in calculating the amount to be paid in any given currency. This was called 'stichometry' in Greek Antiquity and is known as 'casting off' to post-modern printers. Clearly 'stichometry' or 'casting off' is no less important than 'calligraphy' or 'typography' whenever one has in mind a full mastery and control over all the aspects of making and shaping written words into a book format.

In the days of Villon, pricking and ruling had been refined to the extent that, in a way, it was taken over by Gutenberg, together with the letter styles in use at that time. However, the actual prickings and rules, which can be seen on all the pages of the finest and oldest manuscripts, got lost in the process known today as 'imposition'. I do not know what it was called in the days of

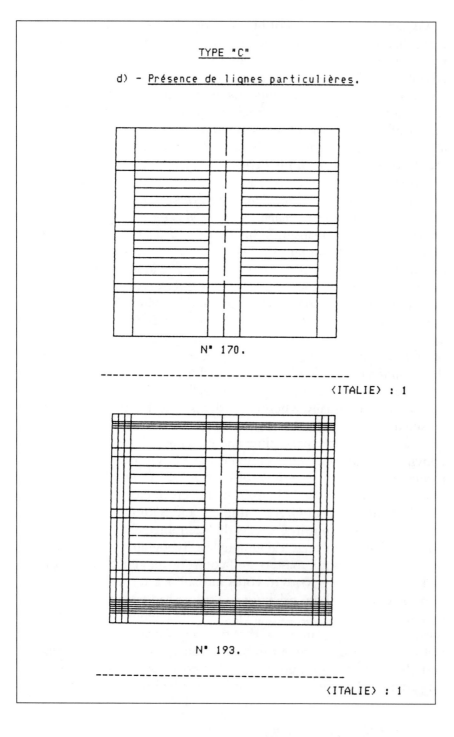

TYPE "C"

d) – Présence de lignes particulières.

N° 170.

⟨ITALIE⟩ : 1

N° 193.

⟨ITALIE⟩ : 1

Figure 1.
These illustrations are taken from Michèle Dukan's *La réglure des manuscrits hébreux du moyen-âge*. Editions du CNRS Paris, 1988. They are reproduced with the kind permission of the author. M. Dukan was of course not concerned with the future of education. Her aim was to classify pricking-systems as a means for identifying, dating and locating medieval manuscripts in general. She inspected 410 Hebrew manuscripts, just as A. Derolez inspected hundreds of Italian humanistic manuscripts.

Figure 2.
When I wanted to know how many alphabets and how many pricking-systems had been applied. The answer was that in the 410 manuscripts inspected 6 different styles of the Hebrew alphabet could be identified, and 157 pricking-systems were distinctly different. This I take as good evidence for my case: arranging letters well is at least as important as the letters themselves. This is what Edward Johnston re-introduced in the teaching of writing and lettering. This is, I feel, what should be re-introduced wherever writing is taught: with or without a pen; with or without a P.C.

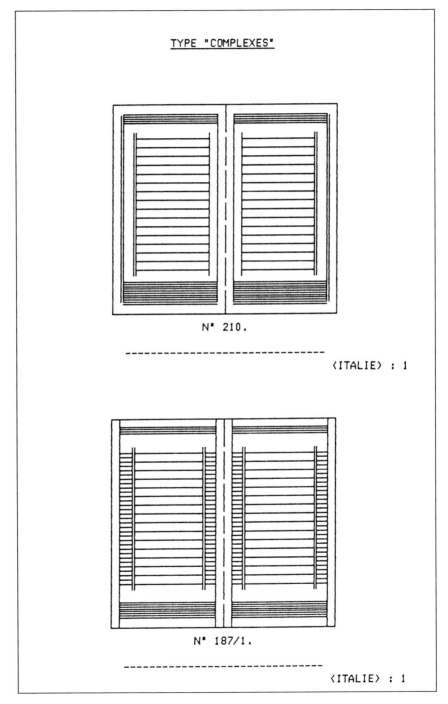

TYPE "COMPLEXES"

N° 210.

⟨ITALIE⟩ : 1

N° 187/1.

⟨ITALIE⟩ : 1

Villon, Gutenberg, Fust and Schöffer, but I do know that it, in the words of Moxon (1683) consisted in 'placing the written pages that belong to a sheet *with the chase and furniture about them* (my italics). in such an order as when the sheet is folded into a quire, all the pages come into an orderly succession'. This know-how was familiar to all the students of the Sorbonne and wherever stationers such as Maître Ferrebouc could be seen working all day, while the students themselves were presumably copying by night or between courses:

Je luy donne ma libraire	I bequeath him my library
Et le Rommant du Pet au Deable	And the Rommant du Pet au Deable
Lequel maistre Guy Tabarie	Which master Guy Tabarie,
Grossa, qui est homme veritable	A truthful man engrossed,
Par cayers est soubz une table.	Its *quires* lay under some table.
etc. *Le Testement*, LXXXVIII.	(to 'engross' was a synonym of copying)

A quire is the folded result of the 'imposition' of a written or printed sheet. The chase and furniture were designed in such a way that they left no trace on the recto or verso of the printed sheet. That is how and why Gutenberg may be said to have obliterated an essential part of a proper education in literacy, even while he was perpetuating its results at the very time when the visual quality of the written word in the West was at its zenith. I referred to Villon first because his ballads are to be found everywhere even in English translation as a Penguin book. Much less accessible is Hartmann Schedel's *Fasciculus temporum*. In his *The Nurenberg Chronicle*, Adrian Wilson describes and reproduces the 'exemplar' and the printed version. No Latin is needed today in order to see that the compositors (1492) had as much Latin as the author and the copist: in the printed version every line has by far more abbreviations in order to fit the line count and to ensure a close and even spacing. It is also worth mentioning that the roman alphabet of the 'exemplar' becomes an Italian gothic in the printed version.

It looks very much as if the 'imposing' of manuscripts resulted from the method known as the 'pecia', as described by Destrez

(1935). It was introduced or inaugurated in the earliest medieval universities in order to facilitate and accelerate the multiplication of, hopefully, identical copies of any given text or 'exemplar'. In this method the *quires* of the exemplars were left unbound and uncut in order to be distributed simultaneously between any number of copyists (also known to Fremin and to any other student or amanuemsis at the Sorbonne in the fifteenth century). We know how imposition works in the press room. There the *raison d'être* of imposition is that it makes it possible for the pressman to print all the recto pages and all the verso pages of a leaf in two press-runs only. First, what Moxon describes as the White Paper Form; second, what he describes as 'Reteration'. Since plano manuscripts have come down to us, I submit that the so-called 'imposition' of manuscripts resulted from the fact that the scribe did not copy the pages of the exemplar in numerical order. He would unfold the exemplar and first copy the recto pages and then the 'reteration', i.e. the verso pages. This way he would turn around the exemplar and the sheet only twice for the recto and twice for the verso, regardless of the number of pages – instead of turning the sheet and the exemplar at the end of every page. My point, at this stage, is that any student in any fifteenth century university knew all that there was to know about the making and shaping of written words in any format, including the book format as the most articulate and elaborate one. To put it mildly, this is more than can be expected of any student and educator today. This implies that a student knew more about 'human speech in spoken and written word' than most printers ever did. Witness what Moxon had to say about the typographer as distinct from the printer. After having reflected on the teachings of Dr Dee, Vitruvius, Leo Battista and Plato, he came to the following conclusion which is, in full, the passage of which I already paraphrased a fragment:

> For my own part, I weighed it well in my thoughts, and find all the accomplishments, *and some more* (my italics), of an architect necessary to be a Typographer . . . By a Typographer I do not mean a Printer, as he is vulgarly accounted, any more than Dr Dee means a carpenter or a mason to be an Architect; but by a Typographer, I mean such a one, who by his own

judgement, *from solid reasoning with himself,* can either perform, *or direct others to perform* (my italics) from the beginning to the end, all the Handyworks and Physical Operations relating to Typographie.

Very few people known to me can get away with that kind of corporate self-esteem. Since Gutenberg himself was never heard, Moxon comes first in chronological order. Next come Fournier, Bodoni and Goudy who make up, together with Moxon, a category of their own. However, one should not forget two archi-typographers totally ignored by Moxon. The first is Christopher Plantin, who was designated as such by his Sovereign, Philip II. The second was known as such only in the mind of William Laud, and described in Barker (1978). As Chancellor of Oxford University he had made a provision in his statutes for 'a Learned Architypographus . . . whose tasks should be the superintendence of paper, presses and type, down to the width of margins and the correction of corrector's errors'.

> Such a Scientific man was doubtless he who was the first Inventor of Typographie; but I think few have succeeded him in Science, though the number of Founders and Printers do grow very many: Insomuch that *for the easie managing of Typographie* (my italics), the Operators have found it necessary to *devide it into several Trades* (my italics), each of which (in the strictest sense) stand no nearer to Typographie, than Carpentry or Masonry are to Architecture. The several devisions that are made are: First the Master Printer, who is as the Soul of Printing; and all the Work-men as members of that Body governed by that Soul subservient to him, etc.

Since Moxon must be taken very seriously indeed on his chosen subject, let us examine what he says and what he leaves out. And let us see if there is anything of use to educators today. First of all we find he makes a clearcut distinction between the Handyworks and the Mechanick Exercises of the Founders and Printers on the one hand and the education of a Typographer on the other, in full accordance with his chosen subject and the way he goes about it. The title of his book is the *Doctrine of Handyworks Applied to the Art of Printing*. What he leaves out is the Doctrine of the Typographer as an Architect. In his introduction he refers to Dr Dee for further information concerning that subject since, 'His arguments are somewhat copious, and the Original easily procurable in the English Tongue'. As Harry Carter puts it in Davis and Carter (1978), 'Of chief importance in this context is the following passage in Dee's preface(fol. diij) from Vitruvius': "An Architect ought to understand Languages, to be skilfull of Painting, well instructed in Geometrie, not ignorant of Perspective, furnished with Arithmetic, have knowledge of many histories, and diligently heard Philosophers, have skill of Musicke, not ignorant of Physicke, know the aunswerses of Lawyers, and have Astronomie, and the course Celestial, in good knowledge." ' But Harry Carter goes on to quote from Leo-Baptista Alberti. I shall limit myself to one sentence of Plato as quoted by Leo-Baptista Alberti and Moxon: 'And Plato affirmeth, the Architect to be Master over all, that make *any* worke'.

I have good reason to feel a village curate in the midst of Lords and Members of the Royal Society. Therefore I am not suggesting that all you need to do is to follow my advice in order to become one of them. I am not delivering advice. I am merely trying to show my readers the evidence now in front of them on this page. Namely, that a member of the Royal Society, a Hydrographer to the King, the author of two volumes on the art of printing, bears witness to the fact that what is important is not the *art of printing* (my italics), not the Mechanick Exercises, not the Handy-Works, not the tools of the master-printer, the compositor or the press-man, but *learning* and *solid reasoning with one's self* as an architect in making and shaping written words into any format regardless of the tool. As a performer or as a director. And please bear in mind that this is what could be expected of any university student, let alone a master, before Gutenberg.

Let me also draw the attention of my readers to the 'easier managing of Typographie' which never ceased to be made easier until now; to the 'deviding into several trades' which went on and on with the appearance of ever new tools for that purpose, until one day – today – all you need is, apparently, a keyboard and a screen. However, even in the days of Moxon, three centuries after Gutenberg, one century after Plantin, van Bomberghen, Garamond, Granjon et al., the pricking, the ruling and the

152

PARTIE II.
CHAP. I.

*INSTRUCTION
pour plier les Im-
positions.*

Prémierement , on
pose cette feuille d'une
maniere qu'on ait les
pages en longueur de-
vant soi, & la signature
seule à main gauche ,
ensuite on plie la feuille
directement aux trous
des pointures, còmme
à l'In-folio ; on prend
ensuite le bout de la
feuille du côté des poin-
tures pour faire rencon-
trer l'extremité de la
derniere ligne de la pa-
ge 12. sur l'autre extre-
mité de la page 13.
aprés quoi on passe le
plioir

LA SCIENCE PRATIQUE

L'In-octavo par feuille entiere.

Figure 3.
These illustrations are
taken from Dominique
Fertel's *La science pratique
de l'Imprimerie Saint-
Omer,* 1723. They
reproduce *two* imposed
forms as they were
prepared for printing
the recto and the verso
of *one* plano sheet.
When folded, the page
numbers fall into
orderly succession and
form one quire of 16
pages. Left: the white
paper form. Right: the
retiration. Today this is
as much of a mystery to
teachers, professors and
students as punch
cutting and type-
foundry. It was familiar
to F. Villon, P. Schöffer
and any student prior to
Gutenberg as part of his
education in the mastery
over human speech in
spoken and written
word.

imposing of plano manuscripts were forgotten. Even more so then
the name of the inventor of writing without a pen.

What had become of the author? He had already, according to
Moxon, become a chap who must be reminded of the fact that he
is supposed to know at least as much about 'Spelling, Pointing,
Italicking, Capitalling Breaking etc.' as the compositor and the
corrector, and that a rough copy will not do, etc. This has, of
course, nothing to do with a doctrine for the making and shaping
of anything. It has to do, as shown by Destrez, with human
shortcomings found in the medieval universities, their scribes, their
exemplars and their imposed manuscripts as much as anything else.
However, that is not the point. The point is that there was a
doctrine, i.e. that the people knew what any piece of writing

Figure 4.
As a matter of fact all you need to know about the subject in order to know where you are and where you want to go is stated by Fertel, P. 22: *When a given copy is to be printed, take a sheet of the paper to be printed and fold it as you wish your book to be: f°, 4°, 8° etc.* This is the clue to all the ensuing instructions to be given concerning the visual aspect of any book as a compilation of quires. Here again it is just as well to bear in mind what Edward Johnston declared at the beginning of this century, namely: *After all the problem before us is fairly simple: to make good letters and to arrange them well. To make good letters is not necessarily to «design» them — they have been designed long ago. To arrange letters requires no great art.*

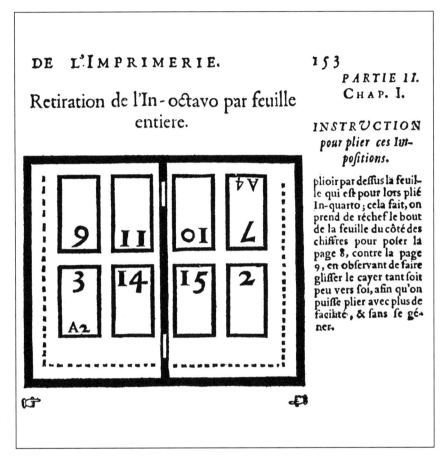

DE L'IMPRIMERIE. 153

Retiration de l'In-octavo par feuille entiere.

PARTIE II.
CHAP. I.

INSTRUCTION pour plier ces Iм-positions.

plioir par deſſus la feuil-le qui eſt pour lors plié In-quarto; cela fait, on prend de réchef le bout de la feuille du côté des chiffres pour poſer la page 8, contre la page 9, en obſervant de faire gliſſer le cayer tant ſoit peu vers ſoi, afin qu'on puiſſe plier avec plus de facilité, & ſans ſe gé-ner.

should look like when they paid the agreed price. They knew what to do and where to go. This is no longer so.

As I said, Moxon was only the first in the chronological order of a category of typographers who set out to describe all the tools of their trade. One of his followers was the Frenchman Dominique Fertel (1684-1752) who described in 1723 in 'La Science Pratique de l'Imprimerie' all that was needed to become a master-printer. He did so after travelling for ten years all over Europe in order to acquire some experience and to collect evidence. He needed 228 pages to illustrate and demonstrate how to compose, i.e. to 'construct' not only title pages but prose pages, bilingual texts or glossed texts. He never mentioned the 'scaffolding', i.e. the pricking and ruling, but he gave the latest examples known to me of some of the practices which had been used in medieval manuscripts. His description of the parts of a press and on the press work takes fewer than 72 pages. His French was somewhat less than literary. He wrote as a printer, not as a man of letters.

The second Frenchman, S. Fournier (1712-68), addressed the men of Letters according to Mosley (1965). Typography was the fashion of the day. The King, *Madame* Pompadour and some courtiers had private presses. In spite of this, S. Fournier discovered that they were talking such typographic nonsense that he decided to put things right. He planned to write four volumes but only two ever got into print: 'The brilliance of Fournier's exposition of punchcutting, typefounding, his point system, his music innovations, his fount schemes, in Vol. I of the Manuel was matched by the display of his types which formed the main part of Vol. II.' James Mosley is the historian; Allen Hutt was the journalist of Fournier's types and publications (1972). However, my point is that typography and the typographer have become synonyms for the mastery by one man of three trades. In the words of Fournier 'Typography . . . may be regarded as consisting of three parts, each "distinct and indispensable, namely, punch cutting, founding and printing . . . only he who combines a knowledge of all three is fit to be styled a typographer.' All Fournier expected from any man of letters, however princely, was to see, with the assistance of a professional, that a given size would fill more space than a smaller one or vice versa. There was no hope for an aristocrat ever to become fit to be styled a typographer – let alone an archi-typographer or architect.

Giambattista Bodoni (1740-1813) had an altogether different approach. In the *Prefazione* he wrote to his *Manuale*, reprinted in Ajani and Maletto (1990), he specified that he had no intention of giving instructions to would-be master-printers: 'I never aspired to any other glory than to revive the good typographic taste . . . the primal typographic simplicity in the finished product'. His *Manuale* is, in fact, what any printer would call a Specimen. It can also be considered as a catalogue, as an exhibition of all the alphabets he ever cut in any number of languages – and that means a lot. As the 'Typographer of Kings and the King of Typographers', he understood that the art of typography would prosper only when its aristocratic or wealthy patrons became connoisseurs. Therefore he suggested that they buy themselves manuscripts and the earliest printed books, known as incunabula. And not only buy them, but study what Bodoni was pleased to call their simplicity.

Needless to say, this aristocratic and costly method is no longer relevant in our democratic age, any more than movable type is. Except that today anyone can be taught right from the beginning, in primary school, how to *look* at any piece of writing – handwritten, typewritten or photocomposed – in order to see how the letters are shaped, how the words are spaced, how the columns are leaded, how the text is articulated and displayed over the space of a page, an ad or a book. He or she will soon be able to see the immense difference between the utter simplicity of Bodoni's layouts and the thoughtful sophistication of medieval manuscripts and early printed books – if only in reproductions. This method is so simple that it can be taught by anyone who can see that the shape of the white spaces is just as important as the form of the letters in any piece of writing or printing. This has been overlooked by most people, including educators at all levels of non-professional schools and art schools ever since pricking and ruling no longer needed to be done.

I realize that I have said very little about the details of ruling and cannot resist just one quotation on this technique from Juan de Yciar's *Arte subtilissima* published in 1550. A facsimile of *Arte subtilissima*, with a translation by Shuckburgh, was published by Oxford University Press in 1960. Yciar says, 'The use of rulers is very important for beginners as will be seen below; and not less for experts who are writing books and other documents in which ruler, compass and square are necessary. Many sorts of rulers have been invented . . . Take a board of beech or walnut and cut upon it as many equidistant straight grooves as you wish to give lines to the paper. In this way you can make many kinds of ruler, large and small, for one or two columns of lines, or in any arrangement. Lay the paper on top of this ruler (made as I described) so it lies square to the strings. Then, holding it so that it does not move out of place, rub it from above, with a cloth until the lute strings make a mark on the paper which emerges ruled as in a mould. This ruler will be sufficient for a whole class and saves one from drawing lines with a lead'.

So much for history. At this stage I think it is just as well to reassure my readers that I am not going to try to put the clock back and to explain how education should redress all the evils of desktop publishing by pricking and ruling as in the good old days. Very far from it, in fact.

Many people have said that Gutenberg 'killed the scribe'. This dramatic language obscures a development which culminated in the early sixties, after five centuries, in what Maximilian Vox described as 'La Mort de Gutenberg' or 'La Révolution du demi-siècle'. Offset and photocomposition had apparently superseded typographic tools once and for all but the first original photocomposing-machine, the Lumitype-Photon, designed by Higonnet and Moyroud, operated for a mere thirty years before it was itself superseded by the computer.

Vox himself explained what he meant by 'La Mort de Gutenburg', namely the disappearance of the chase and furniture which had somehow preserved the scribal know-how for five centuries – incognito, so to speak. This was so much the case that Charles Peignot himself was under the spell of technology to the extent that, in spite of his own experience as a talented layout man and typefounder, he had lost sight of typography as the architecture of the written word. In other words, in the name of typography, typophily and typology he had become an addict to what I would call *typotropism*, i.e. the study of type to the exclusion of space. He was not the first, nor the only one. Of course, he fully understood the essential importance of space and spacing. He knew this better than many so-called professional layout men.

As I.J. Gelb (1952) put it, 'The study of writing from the artistic point of view has heretofore been sadly neglected.' This is true but it is not self-evident in what sense it is true. I.J. Gelb is no longer around, otherwise we should ask him with all due respect exactly what he meant? Especially as he goes on to say, 'The aesthetic feature is sometimes so exaggerated that writing serves the purpose of ornamentation, thus neglecting its primary object of communication; consider for example, Arabic ornamental writing, beautiful but difficult to read, and some exaggerated and baroque uses of writing in modern advertising'. This makes him a follower of Adolf Loos who considered ornamentation a crime. In our so-called post-modern times, is it at least permissible to wonder what I.J.Gelb meant by 'artistic point of view'? And whether he, Loos and any others intolerant of ornament qualify as critics or simply belong to the category of censors? I, for one, have a whole library on the art of the book, the art of printing, type design, graphic design, not to mention books on the history of writing, codicology, etc. apparently unknown or unacceptable to the late I.J.Gelb and kindred spirits. Therefore when I say that in spite of them it is true that the study and the teaching of writing 'have therefore been badly neglected', I must clarify what I mean. I do so as a modest conclusion to my piecemeal and erratic investigation of manuscripts and incunabula.

Recently the computer has entered the primary school of the village where I live. This means that some pupils started using their parent's PCs to do their homework. The headmistress has no official instructions concerning the subject. But she will have none of this and insists that homework be handwritten. However limited this is first hand information. Not just a compilation of what can be found in books and articles. These are all we have to go by concerning the past. But where the future of education is the theme, the live experience of one community is far more valuable than any idealogical day dreaming. In any case her words came nicely in support of my thesis which is: that education in the making and shaping of written words should replace whatever has been taught for the past century as different things, namely, as handwriting, typesetting, calligraphy and typography. This should be done if only because Sampson said nearly fifty years ago, 'A sound educational system must be based on the great means of human intercourse – human speech in spoken and written word' and definitely not on the handling of a number of unrelated tools and the mimicking of any particular model. This means that, whatever the contents of the curriculum, the emphasis should be on clear, distinct articulate speech in spoken *and written* word. Not just in primary school, in professional schools, art schools, but throughout any course of studies. If the word democracy has still any meaning at all, it implies that everyone must be given an equal opportunity to know all there is to know about articulate speech and articulate writing. It has been done in the past without the assistance of the computer. Now, with all the assistance provided by this 'wonderfully inventive age', we should be able to make an even better job.

Whatever I have said and quoted so far does not answer all the questions of education. Of course not. But I am pretty sure that it goes a long way in meeting the much larger issue of the proper attitude to adopt in order to overcome the prevailing sense of chaos, at least in the field of education. Right from the beginning, I have tried to raise the question in my readers' minds: what does he mean by making and shaping written words? And how is it to replace handwriting, calligraphy, typography, etc. as they have been taught so far.

As I said earlier, the prevailing sense of chaos is due to the computer assisted disappearance of all the professional markers and bearings which gave us a sense of security, but which also worked as blinkers and partitions. We could not see the wood for the trees. Now we can. I have given all the historical and actual evidence of another Gutenberg effect: the progressive erosion of any global apprehension of articulate inscriptions as distinct from graffiti. There are any number of degrees between these two extremes. There are no longer any *a priori* partitions. The difference between graffiti and an inscription is not only in the helpless letterforms, it is also in the absence of any definite space. This is so in the case of one letter «I» cut in wood or slate, as well as in the case of the Behistun inscription or the latest edition of the Bible. A vertical bar can be scrawled or very deliberately drawn with a ruler and compass. It takes a dot on top, scrawled or very deliberately drawn with the same tools to look like an 'I'. But this is not enough to make it into an inscription. Anyone who can make a finished Roman capital 'I' will also give a definite shape to the space intended for its inscription. In the case of the Bible, things are much easier today than they were in the days of Plantin – or in the early and late middle ages, for that matter. Today one can – but need not – produce a new alphabet for every new edition. One can pick and choose from any number of the available ready-made alphabets. However, a new grid, new instructions, new correlations have to be made afresh to meet the requirements of the chosen format, the expectations of a particular readership and to stay within the limits of a given budget. Even ready-made alphabets are not on tap. A book format is not to be filled like a paint pot. It takes some solid reasoning.

The so-called 'grid' is the modern equivalent of the medieval pricking and ruling, (see Hurlburt, 1979). The grid has been familiar to graphic designers and book designers ever since the fifties when the Swiss style was so trendy that even in Paris it was enough, if not essential, to be a Swiss in order to be a success as a graphic designer. In spite of that, in Paris at least, not every Swiss had anything like the talent of Albert Hollenstein. I do not know whether or not the Swiss thought they invented the grid, all I know is that no Swiss ever made an allusion to the pricking systems of medieval manuscripts. In any case, they put to shame Stéphane Mallarmé and Orson Welles – Harry Lime who said that the Swiss had never invented anything except the cuckoo clock. Generations of would-be graphic designers flocked to Basle and Zurich from all parts of the world, including America.

I have good reasons for not taking over the turgid terminology and phraseology of the seventeenth century Royal Society which quoted Plato, Vitruvius, Leo Battista and Dr Dee. Not that my subject is less important. On the contrary, I would say it has never been more important to more people than on the threshold of this so-called computer era. Alphabets as metal type are no longer the preserve of a caste of printers. They can no longer be passed on mindlessly together with all the chases and furniture which no one understood what to do with. They were all that was left of the imposition of manuscripts as a method for the efficient and articulate transcription of crude notes into a proper book form.

Handwriting can no longer be taught as a menial task unfit for the elite, to be replaced – the sooner the better – by the computer or another contraption in this 'wonderfully inventive age'. 'Contrarywise'!

> *Much would be gained by substituting, generally,* writing, *for designing* because *writing,* being the medium by which our letters have been evolved, the use of the pen – essentially the lettermaking tool – gives a practical insight into the construction of the letters attainable in no other way . . .
>
> *Ordinary Writing* and even scribbling has had and still might have a good influence on the art of the Letter maker. . . .
>
> After all, the problem before us is fairly simple – *To make good letters and to arrange them well.* To make good letters is not necessarily to design them – they have been designed long ago

. . . To arrange letters well requires no great art, but it requires a working knowledge of letter forms to suit every circumstance.

These citations are from Edward Johnston's Preface to his book on writing, illuminating and lettering. The presence of illuminating should not mislead anyone into thinking that Johnston was a medievalist or passeist. Far from it:

Edward Johnston designed the first of the important twentieth century sans serifs. This influential type was commissioned by London Underground Railways in 1916 and named 'Underground' . . . The London design group Banks and Miles, undertook a complete review of London Transport's publicity in 1979. As a part of that activity Colin Banks (b. 1932) revived the use of the typeface by redesigning it and producing a new family of eight "weights".

What these citations of Johnston and this comment on his 'Underground' illustrate is that even a huge amount of knowledge of the past has never been an obstacle to 'suiting every circumstance', however modern or post-modern it may be. We are witnessing what happens only seventy years after a deliberate attempt had been made to cut off the past. The nearest PC has at least one lesson for you: without memory it is useless.

The history and development of printing presses from the fifteenth century to modern times is far more spectacular than the history and development of typefaces during the same period. Moran (1973) looks at this development during this time. Needless to say the evolution since 1973 has been even more spectacular. The history and development of composing machines is coming to a close after only one century. More ready-made alphabets are now available to a child at home than most printers could buy in a lifetime and accommodate in their workshops. In the days of hot metal it took five years for an apprentice to learn how to follow the instructions of his overseer concerning the titles and the text, the sizes of type, the measure of the line, the number of lines per page. So it was in Belgium in the sixties. It took another number of years for the apprentice to learn how to make up a forme, i.e. how to place (impose) any number of pages and the needed furniture corresponding to a given size of paper and a given press. The professional training of a pressman was yet another lengthy affair. All he knew was how to work together with the others in the composing room and the press room. Not one of them, however, knew anything about what Moxon may have been the last to describe as 'typographie', meaning the 'architecture' of human speech in written words. Nor should anyone suppose that the authors and publishers knew any more or any better. Quite the contrary, especially in the case of the authors. They did not see the letterforms even while using them if only as readers. They never realized that someone was also responsible for the margins. Except, of course, those who were concerned with fine printing. But Fine Printing is no answer to the situation created by desk top publishing. No amount of fine type in the memory of a computer is of any use if there is no corresponding amount of 'typographie' in the memory of the human hand, the human eye and the human brain.

Education in the two great means of human intercourse – human speech in spoken and written word – was deflected from its natural course as soon as Gutenberg dissociated them and initiated the spectacular technological progress. Quite recently this technological progress has quite unexpectedly and physically eliminated all the tools traditionally associated with 'writing without a pen'. This, at least to me, is a clear indication that 'writing' is more than a particular tool, model, method, system, medium, alphabet or other graphic system. I am afraid – *pace* Sampson – that writing has become as abstract in secular terms as it ever was in the Beginning when it was all Holy Writ. However I was not there at the Beginning. All I know is that we are, all of us, right at the beginning of the so-called computer era. Especially as educators. First of all we should avoid putting the cuckoo-clock back, or bashing it to pieces. Then we should be able, at long last, to try to learn and to teach how to do a bit of solid reasoning whenever we have recourse to such abstract means of human intercourse as human speech, especially in written words. Also let us stop talking about handwriting, calligraphy, typewriting, typography as if they were separate subjects. They are one and the same subject – writing as a means to an end. Too much has been written about writing as a record of the past. Writing, in combination with drawing, is the best method known to humankind for planning whatever needs planning. Instead of opposing the written word and the pictures, I think it is more helpful to see the written word as a picture in its own right.

And now we can start talking about how to teach 'typographie' as distinct from *typotropism*. The difference is, of course, that instead of thinking exclusively in terms of any number of more or less articulate letterforms, we take into account the more or less articulate space as well. As a picture, writing is deceptively simpler than any other painting, engraving, movie, etc. It always consists in any number of letterforms in any number of sizes (what I call a 'constellation of alphabets') and in any number of lines arranged in columns (what I call a 'configuration of texts'). That's all. Well, more or less. . .

The quality of any piece of writing is measured by the degree of precision intended and achieved in the letterforms and in their spacing. The trouble with the computer is that many of the available and ready-made alphabets achieve such a degree of precision, and are so attractive as a result, that even educators may be tempted to jump to the conclusion that it is simpler and more gratifying to use them. This is a mistake. With or without a computer, the human hand, the human eye, the human brain must be trained together in order to spot the particular talent of any child. Otherwise, instead of educating, you are mutilating.

To stop training any one of the three at any stage is just as mutilating since that too denies a free choice. An ignoramus can make no free choice. And there is ever more to learn in order to be styled a 'typographer', as we learn from Moxon. (The phrase is Fournier's but the lesson is Moxon's).

Where do we begin? By training teachers first. They should know where to look in order to see how the constellations of alphabets and the configurations of text combine in a given space and are shaped in any format – broadsheet, poster, brochure, book, etc. that may be lying around. Teachers need to be made aware of what must be done in an advertisement, a magazine, which cannot be done in a dictionary, an encyclopedia, a timetable or a signage system. It is far from enough simply to make them type-conscious, as my readers may have realized by now. They must be space conscious as well. (A method for doing this will be described and illustrated in *L'Effet Gutenberg*).

Here I.J.Gelb's verdict applies almost verbatim: 'The study of writing from the Moxonian point of view has heretofore been sadly neglected.' At least this is true for compulsory education. Not by commission or omission. It is due to the circumstances I have investigated and, hopefully, made clear. Hermann Zapf reportedly taught himself all he needed to know to become Hermann Zapf by reading Johnston's *Writing & Illuminating & Lettering*. It does not always work that way. There have always been plenty of books from which one can teach oneself anything. Many people do. But all this has nothing to do with compulsory education as an establishment.

Let me draw one more conclusion before the final one. Just as there is a clear distinction to be made between writing and the tools designed to multiply or transmit any given piece of writing such as it is, there is also a clear distinction to be made – so it seems to me – between the *linguistic grammar* that makes the sense (or nonsense) and the far simpler *visual grammar* that makes up writing – any piece of writing as a picture, provided it is duly centred and in focus. Whether all the operations involved in the *grammatical editing* or the *visual editing* are made by one person in one place, or by any number of people spread all over the planet, is irrelevant. Only the tuning in of the visual and the grammatical is important. 'Tuning in' is just another phrase for education – generally and compulsory.

I would not be surprised to learn that no establishment has ever heard of the Moxonian point of view (as defined by Baudin), or that nothing whatsoever has been published from that particular point of view. I believe it is worth considering by anyone who is in the business of . . . whatever. It would be a good beginning indeed for the updating of education generally if all teachers could be made aware of the role of spacing in any piece of writing – not only in primary school but for the rest of one's life.

It is not essential that everyone acquire a full coordination of the hand and eye and brain. Very few ever achieve this. It takes more than can be taught in school. The important thing is to know and to teach that handwriting, not the computer, is a root of democracy and rational thought.

References

Adam, Comte Villiers de l'Isle, (1891). *L'Ève Future. Bibliothèque Charpentier.*

Ajani S. and Maletto L.C. (1990). *Conoscere Bodoni. Gianfranco Altieri Editore, Centro Culturale St. Vincent.*

Banks and Miles (1991) in *26 Letters, Lettern, Lettres.* An international cooperation of typedesigners and typemanufacturers. 1992.

Barker N. (1978). The Oxford University Press and the Spread of Learning. Clarendon Press p.11

Baudin F. (1984). *La Typographie au Tableau Noir.* Edition Retz. Translated (1988) as *How Typography Works and Why it is Important.* Lund Humphries.

Baudin F. (1966). *Stanley Morison et la tradition typographique.* Exposition: Bibliothèque Albert Ire Bruxelles, Belgium. Rijksmuseum, Meermanno-Westreenianumgs-Graven hage. The Netherlands.

Baudin F. *L'Effet Gutenberg.* To be published by *Le Cercle de la Libraire.* Promidis, Paris.

Berry T and Poole H.E. (1966). *Annals of Printing.* Blandford Press.

Davis H. and Carter H. (1978). *Joseph Moxon, Mechanick Exercises on the Whole Art of Printing.* Dover Publications.

Destrez J. (1935). *La Pecia dans les Manuscrits Universitaires du XIIIe et du XIVe Siècle.* Edition Jacques Vautrain.

Eisenstein E. (1970). *The Printing Press as an Agent of Change.* 2 vols. Cambridge University Press.

Gelb I.J. (1952). *A Study of Writing.* A Phoenix book. The University of Chicago Press.

Hellinga L. (1989). *Analytical Bibliography and Study of Early Printed Books With a Case Study of Mainz Catholicon, in Gutenberg Jahrbuch* pp. 47-97.

Hurlburt A. (1979). *The Grid. A Modular System for the Design and Production of Newspapers, Magazines and Books.* Barrie and Jenkins.

Hutt A. (1972). *Fournier the Compleat Typographer.* Frederick Muller.

Johnston E. (1906). *Writing & Illuminating & Lettering.* Pitman.

Loos A. (1979). *Paroles dans la vide* (1898) and *Malgré tout* (1900-1913) éditions *Champs Libre.*

McLuhan, M. (1962). *The Gutenberg Galaxy.* University of Toronto Press

Mialaret G. and Vial J. (1981). *Histoire Mondiale de l'Éducation. Presses Universitaires.* Vol. III, p.239.

Moran J. (1973). *Printing Presses, History and development from the fifteenth century to Modern Times.* Faber and Faber.

Mosley J. (1965). *An Introduction to Pierre Fournier's Modèles des Caractères de l'Imprimerie. Introduction to collotype facsimile.* Eugramma Press.

Moxon J. (1683). *Mechanick Exercises Or the Doctrine of Handy-works Applied to the Art of Printing.*

Poe E.A. (1989). *The Man Who Was Used up. In Poetry and Tales, The Library of America,* p307.

Whitehouse J.H. (1945). *Ruskins's Influence Today.* Oxford University Press.

Zapf, H. & His Design Philosophy (1987) Society of Typographic Arts, Chicago.

ALAN MARSHALL

A typographer
by any other name

IT IS DOUBTLESS a somewhat banal remark to make in this post-modern world, but the printed word is not what it used to be. Technical and economic changes have taken place which would have been unimaginable for the average printer twenty years ago – particularly in the field of text composition where rapidly accelerating computerization has relegated hot metal and several generations of phototypesetting machines to no more than a distant memory. But if there can be little doubt about the importance of the changes which have taken place, their exact significance for the long-term future of typography is often rather more difficult to ascertain in the welter of claims and counter-claims made by the partisans and critics of the various techniques involved. Certainly the machines have changed, as has the organization of what might more globally be called 'typographical production'. But in an industry in which the life of each generation of machines is counted in months rather than years, the woods are often obscured by the trees and the most absurdly futurist or reactionary arguments are often taken at face value. Have the new personal computer-based techniques fundamentally diminished the role of the typographical specialist as their promoters once claimed they would? Has the printed word irremediably suffered at the hands of computer engineers as typographical purists feared?

It is not, of course, unusual for technical innovation to be accompanied by a certain confusion as to its true significance. New technologies are seldom, if ever, born overnight, despite what manufacturers repeatedly try to tell us. It is one thing to build a new machine (even a 'revolutionary' one). It is quite another to say how it is going to find its place in industry or what place it will ultimately occupy in society. New techniques inevitably go through a period during which their uses and the markets for their products define themselves and stabilize.

In the case of what used to be known as type composition, the various generations of machines have followed each other at a vertiginous rate since the late 1940s. Four generations of phototypesetting systems and the introduction, first of general-purpose computers, then of word processors and, finally, of desktop publishing, have progressively dissolved the frontiers between the various hitherto well-defined stages of editorial, typesetting and printing activities. However, these changes are not simply the result of technological innovation. They are also the result of economic and cultural changes such as the decline of traditional taylorist forms of work organization, the acceleration of information production and consumption cycles, and the multiplication and fragmentation of the ways in which the printed word is used. In order to appreciate the likely long-term evolution of an activity as complex as typography, it is important to consider not only the extent to which new techniques constitute a break with the past, but also to what extent their industrial development is conditioned by non-technical factors. For typography is not simply a technical activity; it is profoundly rooted in past and present social and cultural practices.

The decline of hot metal

The traditional conception of typographical production, as it had been slowly built up over five centuries, first began to be seriously eroded in the 1950s with the introduction of first and second generation phototypesetters in which molten lead was replaced by light. Instead of casting individual letters in hot metal (like the Monotype) or complete lines of type (Linotype), they photo-graphed text onto light-sensitive film or paper using a light source and a set of negative film-masters.

Phototypesetting is often – wrongly – thought of as the first step in the dematerialization of the letter. Certainly the replacement of metal casting techniques by photography – the result of over half a century of experiments – was a momentous step forward for the printing industry, opening as it did the door to the rational exploitation of computers in text assembly. However, hot metal techniques had already been moving towards dematerialization. By introducing a system which used a limited number of matrices (moulds from which the letters were cast), the Linotype and Monotype machines had already eliminated the need for tons of costly traditional founder's type. In both cases there was a shift away from the handling of material objects towards the processing of information. In the Linotype, the identity of each letter was encoded in a series of notches on the corresponding matrix. With the Monotype, the identity of the letters and their sequence in the assembled character string was encoded on punched tape which was then used to operate a casting machine.

The replacement of hot metal by photography was thus only a step in the process which had been started in the late nineteenth century and which had gathered momentum in the late thirties with the introduction of the teletypesetter (a punched tape system used to increase the productivity of linecasters and to transmit encoded typeset matter by telephone lines). It was, however, a crucial step, for the abandonment of hot metal circumvented the speed barrier imposed by the need to cool the molten lead during the casting process, thus radically increasing the potential productivity of typesetting operations.

The next step in the dematerialization of the letter was to replace the photographic system of letter storage used by first and second generation machines by an electronic storage system. In third and fourth generation machines the letter lost its last vestiges of materiality, becoming a geometrical description stored electronically in binary digital form. The effect of this was not only further to increase the speed of typesetting operations, it undermined the very notion of typesetting, for text and and images could now be handled together within the same system. Digital 'imagesetters' could now handle all the information necessary for the production of any imaginable kind of printed product.

On a more concrete level, traditional printers were also threatened by a new sector which was developing on the margins of the traditional printing industry. In-plant printing or, more generally, reprographics, was based on a series of new (and not so new) techniques hitherto little-used in conventional print shops – justifying typewriters, word processors, daisy wheel printers, photocopiers, small offset duplicators and electrostatic or chemical diffusion platemaking systems. Thanks to the growth in the market for so-called 'information printing' in the sixties and seventies, repro-graphics rapidly became an autonomous sector within the graphic industries with its own equipment and product markets and its own industrial dynamic.

The introduction of such low-cost, flexible technologies was removing one of the main obstacles which had hitherto limited entry into the printing trade – namely the high cost of special-purpose machines such as the Linotype and the industrial printing press. Equipped with a justifying typewriter and a small offset duplicator, everyone and his dog was getting into printing. Even worse, they were often producing decent results!

But the new reprographics sector was not the only threat to the livelihood of traditional printers. They also had to face up to the progressive encroachment of data processing in the typographical domain; for the 1960s also saw the first steps towards the merging of two areas of text processing which had up until then remained quite separate – data processing and composition. The first patents covering the use of a general-purpose digital computer for the purposes of typesetting were taken out by the BBR syndicate in France in 1954 and several years later the Photon Corporation began working with a team of computer scientists at MIT with a view to building the first computer-driven slave phototypesetter.

Thus in the face of unrelenting technological change and the emergence of new in-plant competitors in the administrative sector, traditional printers began to feel seriously threatened. Computing departments of large firms and administrations were becoming major sources of texts destined to be printed, and users of mainframe systems were looking increasingly to the typograph-ical quality of their output with a view to improving legibility and saving paper. At the same time, word processors were finding their way into more and more offices and the race was on to render them compatible with phototypesetting systems in order to elimi-nate the wasteful rekeying of data which already existed in electronic form.

The result of these various technical initiatives was a deepening malaise within the printing industry. The telescoping of several hitherto separate techniques implied a massive reorganization of typographical production and a radically new approach to training and skills. Printers' metaphysical angst quickly took a more concrete form – that of industrial unrest – as the moment of truth approached when unions and management would have to come to an agreement as to how the new techniques should be introduced and for whose benefit. The printing industry had entered a crisis which was to last twenty years and which was to culminate in the introduction of desktop publishing in the late eighties.

However, contrary to popular opinion, desktop publishing was not so much a breakthrough in technical or economic terms as in organizational and cultural terms. If at first glance that seems an odd thing to say, it should be borne in mind that many of the basic technical principles of desktop publishing were already known to printers – integrated digital text/image composition systems (albeit very expensive ones!) were already in use in the printing industry, as were laser printers and more or less interactive page make-up terminals. Much more important than the (not insignificant, but often exaggerated) economic gains were the substantial increases in organizational flexibility and typographical performance which desktop publishing brought to 'non-professional' methods of type composition. The abandonment of explicit coding in favour of (more or less) WYSIWYG operation rendered typography 'accessible' to non-specialists. There was often a loss in production speed and precision, and the result was not necessarily good typography, but for most people it was a considerable advance over the typewriter. Also, for the first time in history, secretaries, managers, technicians, writers and academics could use the same basic equipment as the printer. It was no longer necessary to invest in tons of foundry type or a Linotype and a printing press to escape from the inevitable air of confidentiality which the humble typewriter had hitherto imposed on the 'non-printed' printed word.

In the end, the traditional printing industry survived the combined efforts of reprographics, data processing and desktop publishing to put it out of business – though not without considerable disruption. And now that the initial enthusiasm for the automation of typographical production and its corollary, the elimination of the skilled compositor, has died down, it is at last becoming obvious to everyone concerned that good typography needs imagination and skill as much as sophisticated machines and software. Paradoxically, rather than putting an end to typography as a skilled activity, the new user-friendly technologies are in the process of revalorizing it by opening up the intricate mechanics of text and page assembly to a much wider audience. Similarly, the new desktop publishers are becoming increasingly aware of the role of so-called 'traditional' skills in typography.

However, though there are strong reasons to believe that the skilled typographer will remain a key element in the production of the printed word, the exact form which the evolution of the 'typographical trades' is likely to take is rather less easy to discern. For if it is hard to imagine a renaissance of traditional forms of skilled print labour organization, it is equally difficult to imagine that the new typographers of the Macintosh generation will resist the temptation to create new professional structures in order to defend their identity and collective interests within the all-encompassing miasma of the 'communications industries'.

Apocalypse now, apocalypse then

Before trying to determine to what extent desktop publishing constitutes a true break with the typographical practices of the past, it is perhaps worth taking a few lines to put recent arguments about the computerization of typographical production in some kind of historical context. For the fervent arguments for and against desktop publishing are nothing new. Over the last century and a half, every major technological innovation has provoked heated arguments about the future of the printed word. Optimists have embraced new techniques as a means to increase productivity and open up new markets, while pessimists have seen little more than unemployment, de-skilling, falling quality and the devalorization of literacy skills and the printed word generally.

At the end of the nineteenth century, it was the mechanization of type composition which provoked heated reactions. The introduction of the Linotype and Monotype machines profoundly destabilized the trade over a period of ten years during which time large numbers of compositors found themselves out of work, replaced either by the 'iron comp' or, to a lesser extent, by low-paid women operators. Similarly, the new composing machines threatened the traditional markets of type founders', especially in the book and newspaper fields.

The print unions, led by a small number of their leaders, quickly realized that it was impossible to avoid job losses in the short term, and adopted a strategy based on gaining control of the new techniques in order to reinforce their position within the trade in the long term. Thus when print production took off again and the employers finally recognized that it was usually a false economy to employ 'typists' instead of skilled compositors, the unions found themselves once again in a position of strength. Such a strategy was implicitly based on the recognition that increased productivity would help promote growth in print markets. Which indeed turned out to be the case.

From a typographical point of view, the main concern of manufacturers such as Linotype and Monotype was initially to perfect their machines mechanically so that they would meet the demands of printers. So long as their machines could set type straight and relatively well-spaced at a lower price than could be done by hand, they gave little attention to the quality of the letters. Their aim was simply to get into the existing market and to compete with hand setting on its own ground. It was only much later, when competition began to hot up within the newly-established mechanical typesetting market (the Intertype, a Linotype 'clone' began to find its way into composing rooms just after the First World War) that they began seriously to improve the quality of their typography.

This time-lag between the commercial implementation of a new technique and its full exploitation in æsthetic terms is typical of periods of major technological change. The first effect of the introduction of a new technique is to use the resulting productivity gains to increase the output of existing products. Only later do product innovations appear – when hitherto patented techniques begin to fall into the public domain and when increases in the volume of production are no longer sufficient to maintain a lead in the market. Firms then look for new ways in which to harness their technical resources to social and cultural needs through new products and markets. The invention of printing in the fifteenth century is an excellent example of this process. The first types used by Gutenberg and his contemporaries were exactly based on existing forms of writing used by scribes. Printers were thus able to insert their 'new' printed products easily into existing markets without having to create new forms of demand.

In the case of mechanical type composition, the introduction of the Linotype and the Monotype at first provoked angry outbursts from many traditional printers who feared a serious degradation of typographic standards – on the one hand because of the loss of the traditional skills of the hand compositor, and on the other because of the deformations imposed on letters by Linotype's system of duplexation (putting two essentially different types of letter – roman and italic for example – on a single matrix of fixed width). In the end it was nearly forty years before the new process was fully exploited – from the first prototype machines in the 1880s, until the 1920s, when Linotype and Monotype seriously embarked on the creation of new typefaces (albeit for the most part adaptations of known typeforms to modern tastes and production conditions).

However, at the beginning of the century the traditions of the printing industry were not only periodically threatened by the disruption which accompanied the introduction of new processes (offset litho and rotogravure were also developing rapidly). An even more revolutionary idea was beginning to take root – that of a 'post-typographical' society. Apollinaire, for example, considered that still photography and the cinema would soon sound the death knell for typography. Similarly, in post-revolutionary Russia, El Lissitsky and others were planning a radiant future in which the masses, particularly the younger generation, would be able to educate and entertain themselves without having to go through the arduous process of reading. Printed and moving images as well as the radio would 'dematerialize' and 'democratize' the means of mass communication. Lissitsky was right in thinking that the means of communication were going to change radically in the years to come and that audio-visual media were going to play an increasing role. But the demise of text was not yet on the agenda. On the contrary, book production was to become a truly mass production industry with the advent of the paperback.

The idea of cheap, popular editions had been around for some time (it was, after all, Aldus Manutius who thought up the idea in the first place) and several publishers had already had a certain success in the paperback field before the Lane brothers changed the rules of the game with their Penguin Books. The first batch of ten Penguins was published in 1935. They sold for 6 pence (6d.) a copy, a fifth of the price of a cheap hard back at the time. But the true originality of Penguins lay not in their size, price or form of binding, but in the aggressive attitude adopted by their publishers to marketing. Popular publishing meant mass production. And mass production needed mass marketing to succeed. Penguins were sold, not only in bookshops, but also in such low-class, uncultured establishments as Woolworths. They were even sold in machines like chewing gum! Naturally the lamentations of the defenders of culture were quick to follow. Such a degradation of the status of the book could only lead to catastrophe. George Orwell, for example, took Penguin to task in an article published in the *New English Weekly* in 1936. He argued that the paperback would be bad not only for the reader because of its reduced format and quality, but also for authors, publishers and printers because of reduced profit margins. What Orwell (and others) missed was the elementary commercial principle that reduced margins can be compensated for by market expansion. And if democratizing print culture meant anything at all it meant just that – putting it within reach of a vastly expanded audience. (As for the reduced physical margins on the page, Penguin made up for this by paying particular attention to the typographical quality of its books.)

Given such an illustrious line of precedents, it was hardly surprising that the ideologists of technical progress should once again pour scorn on the printed word in the fifties and sixties. Computers were coming out of the laboratories and into industry, and automation had become the watchword for a new generation. In the light of Shannon and Weaver's information theory and Daniel Bell's vision of a post-industrial society, it again became difficult (at least for the pundits) to imagine how an industry as mechanistic and hide-bound by tradition as printing could survive the coming technical revolution.

To cap it all, the technocrats even had the support of a certain number of literary people. In France the success on an industrial scale of the small-format paperback (twenty years after its appearance in Britain and North America) provoked a minor scandal and the arguments for and against raged in the literary journals for months. And in Canada an academic by the name of Marshall McLuhan was predicting the end of typographical civilization no less! According to McLuhan, audio-visual media were in the process of fragmenting the 'single point of view' which had been the originality of Renaissance civilization and which had dominated Western culture ever since. His argument, which could not fail to seduce the increasingly powerful audio-visual media, was that the 'linear' culture of the printed word would soon have to make way for a richer, more complex culture based on the image.

Although the details of his analysis are now largely forgotten, McLuhan became (and remains) a symbol of the decline of the status of the printed word and of the graphic industries in the face of electronic media. Which is odd, because society has remained resolutely typographical and the printing industry seems to be in no great hurry to lie down and die (despite its reluctance to go to the doctor). McLuhan's analysis was, of course, fuelled by the coming demise of hot metal – the so-called 'death of Gutenberg' – in the face of the rapid advance of phototypesetting and offset litho. However, successive generations of photo- and computer typesetting equipment did not in the end undermine the role of the typographical specialist in the production of the printed word. Certainly they reduced the number of typographical specialists and broke the hegemony of the male craft worker in the composing room. But the high capital cost and complexity of the new machines guaranteed that the bulk of typesetting work did not get done outside the traditional organizational structures of the printing industry. Likewise the abstract nature of the work guaranteed a continuing role for the typographic specialist. If, on the one hand, true compositors were becoming a rarity in many areas of the trade – replaced by semi-skilled 'keyboard operators' – typographical responsibility was, on the other hand, being transferred to an expanding population of designers who were increasingly required to intervene in the nuts and bolts of text and page assembly.

As for the loss in quality which many typographical purists thought would be the only guaranteed result of the abandonment of hot metal, this also has to be put into perspective. The real but often exaggerated loss of quality which followed the introduction of phototypesetting stemmed from two changes. Firstly, the adoption of a single master letterform for all typesizes (and the wave of typeface piracy which accompanied the production of these masters) led to all sorts of distortions and unsightly results.

Secondly, the rapid introduction of new technology into a traditionally stable industry profoundly disrupted training structures and put existing skills increasingly out of phase with technical developments. Cheap photosetting machines made their way into the hands of people who were 'more concerned with the bottom line than with the baseline' – with entirely predictable results.

However it was not the first time that typographical quality had suffered at the hands of technology. In the nineteenth century the introduction of electrotyping opened the way to the pirating of type and to a lowering of standards. Similarly, the Linotype's system of duplexation initially produced results which were just as awful as one commonly sees today. And, fifty years later, the Teletypesetter had the North American press turning typographical somersaults in order to balance cost-cutting with legibility.

But if truth be told, the unfortunate effects of each of these innovations were often relatively marginal when compared with the generally abysmal quality of a sizeable section of the printing industry. For it is pure wishful thinking to imagine that the printing fraternity as a whole has ever been the guarantor of typographical quality. For at least two centuries there had always been a large population of printers for whom good typography had little or nothing to do with good business, and it is not without significance that 'outsiders' have repeatedly been the source of typographical innovation or renovation.

From this brief evocation of some of the better-known periods of technologically-prompted gloom and doom in the printing industry, it can be seen that the predictions which accompanied the latest threat – desktop publishing – were far from new. However, the launching of the concept of desktop publishing as a marketing strategy by Apple in 1985 undoubtedly marked a new low in the morale of many printers. If typographical production slipped out of the control of printers, typographical chaos could not be far behind, with secretaries producing office stationery in every kind of display face imaginable, and do-it-yourself publishers setting Shakespeare in Futura bold! How would the printed word ever survive such a grievous attack by the typographically uneducated?

Paradoxically, desktop publishing threatened neither typographers nor typographic products, despite the marketing propaganda put out by the manufacturers. Desktop publishing, with its expressed aim of democratizing typography, made low-cost typographical tools (or should we say 'writing tools') widely available. Cheap and powerful micro-computers, laser printers and user-friendly software inevitably brought an increasing number of people into direct contact with typography.

However, the idea of 'democratizing typography' frequently put forward by the partisans of desktop publishing is, for two reasons not quite so simple as it appears at first sight, laudable as it undoubtedly is. Firstly, it assumes that the term 'desktop publishing' will have a meaning in the long term (i.e. that in ten years' time it will not just be yet another synonym for text or page assembly). Secondly, in emphasizing the advantages of interactive WYSIWYG working at a particular stage in the development of typographical techniques, it has until now largely left the question of skill unresolved.

Who's doing what?

Desktop publishing was originally viewed by printers as an impending catastrophe. Several years on, however, the Mac and its colleagues have been widely accepted in photosetting shops. Having first provoked the break-up of traditional notions of 'the trade', desktop publishing has now become the driving force behind a global restructuring of editorial activities, text/image processing and page assembly. It has even led to an enlargement of the field of typographical applications. The appearance of a host of desktop publishers in offices, industry, schools and universities is not only a sign of an increased awareness of typography, it has also provided the breeding ground of a new generation of typographers.

There was never any doubt that desktop publishing would have a major impact on typographical activities. However, there was considerable confusion in the early years about exactly what that impact would be. For obvious commercial reasons, manufacturers put the emphasis on the simplicity and user-friendliness of micro-computer-based systems. Traditional phototypesetting systems requiring extensive manual coding and the interpretation of complex visual displays were replaced by much more readily-accessible menu systems while WYSIWYG screens provided instant 'page proofs'. It was but a short step for manufacturers to suggest that typography was a question of software ergonomics rather than traditional typographical skills. Their analysis of production organization was, however, often excessively simplistic. For many manufacturers and users, desktop publishing simply meant the automation of a large section of typographical activities and the elimination of skilled print labour from text and page assembly processes!

Such an analysis was underpinned by an excessively technicist approach to typography. Manufacturers argued that it was enough to have cheap, accessible and versatile machines in order to make massive savings on printing costs. Desktop publishing was fast, data could be readily moved from one system to another, and the integration of text and images was child's play. In order to get their foot in the door of a well-established and highly-structured market, manufacturers skirted round questions of skills, training and organization, minimizing the importance of 'hidden' production costs. Thanks to the minimal cost of personal computers as compared with traditional phototypesetting systems, and the eminently playful nature of WYSIWYG working, they had little difficulty convincing large numbers of firms and individuals to become desktop publishers.

However, for many who launched themselves on a typographical career on the basis of calculations made on the back of an envelope in their local Mac dealer's showroom, it came as a shock when they discovered that there was a lot more to publishing than owning a computer and a laser printer. First of all there were hardware additions of all sorts. Likewise a wide range of basic software was required, as was a scanner to cope with images, and a whole series of specialized applications to streamline production. An increasing amount of time also had to be spent to keep up to date with new developments (if only to fend off the arguments of customers who had a nasty tendency to demand the very latest gadgetry whether ir not it helped in the production process) and in plumbing the depths (and avoiding the bugs) of each successive software version. Then there was training. It was all very well to have machines which could be operated by an educated typist. But typists come and go much faster than skilled compositors, and in the early years they very often lacked a basic grounding in the increasingly complementary areas of computing and typography. Perpetual training schemes take a lot of working out and use up considerable energy.

Thus, as the initial wave of enthusiasm passed and disenchantment set in as regards infinitely elastic working hours and infinitely compressible profit margins, technical considerations gradually gave way to questions of organization, training and quality. On-the-job training was no longer enough and, as traditional typesetters adopted the new techniques, the newcomers urgently had to rationalize their production methods. As for the manufacturers, they were not far behind. The high-tech sales arguments about accessibility and user-friendliness which had allowed them to establish themselves in the market gave way to an increasingly sophisticated discourse based on notions of typographical rigour, quality and skill.

Democratizing typography – myth or reality?

What have been the consequences of all these changes for the democratization of typography? If, on the one hand the machines and the vocabulary have changed, can it also be said that the personal computer and the laser printer have eliminated the skilled typographical worker from the production process? What is it (apart from the technology) that distinguishes desktop publishing from so-called traditional typography?

Typography for the masses is an excellent idea – and not simply from the point of view of computer manufacturers' turnover. Fernand Baudin has frequently pointed out that it is an aberration for typography to be a skill limited to printers. Textual coherence, punctuation, the use of capitals etc., are above all the author's responsibility, not the printer's. It is just as absurd to employ a typographer to ensure the coherence of a text produced by an author as it is in this day and age to employ a compositor to rekey a text which has already been typed by a typist. But, as Fernand Baudin is also the first to point out, so long as writing (in the full sense of the word, i.e. spacing and layout as well as words and punctuation) is not taught at school and at university, most texts produced on micro-computers will never reach the standards necessary for the effective transmission of ideas or information from one person to another (in terms of accuracy or legibility for example) – especially if the communication process is underpinned by a commercial transaction!

Up until now, the claims that the personal computer will

democratize typography have been based largely on the cheapness of the hardware: desktop publishing is, according to popular wisdom, considerably cheaper than traditional typesetting methods. But is this really the case? The most cursory glance would suggest the need for caution.

Cost comparisons are generally made between a basic desktop publishing configuration on the one hand and a sophisticated third or fourth generation phototypesetting system on the other. However, in most cases it would be more appropriate (at least in organizational and market terms) to compare a desktop publishing spread to an IBM composer (or a Varityper) and a paste-up studio. For the status of photosetting output devices is far from clear in most cases. Nowadays most phototypesetters use desktop publishing sytems to feed their photosetting units while at the same time offering their customers plain paper laser proofs (or even definitive output). As for desktop publishers, they no longer limit themselves to 300 dpi laser output. To stay in business, they have to offer what they call 'high-resolution output' (what used to be normal resolution in the old days!) on a photosetting unit. What then should we compare with what? Should we conclude that a photosetter with its RIP form part of a basic desktop publishing configuration? To further complicate matters, dedicated text inputting terminals are increasingly restricted to a few very particular market sectors. Keen to profit from economies of scale, traditional typesetting equipment manufacturers cannot get their software onto (more or less) standard hardware platforms fast enough. The result will be that, as the differences between desktop publishing and traditional phototypesetting equipment disappear, the different typographical markets will be increasingly differentiated by the software and firmware involved and by the skills necessary to use it effectively in normal production conditions. It is essential to bear in mind that the fact that typographical work is now carried out using standard production-line computers instead of dedicated machines does not in any way reduce the diversity of the printed word's uses and markets, a diversity which has been steadily increasing over that last century. Given that traditional phototypesetters have been unable to cover the full range of typographical products (each specializing in one or other of its chosen sectors), it is unlikely that the new desktop publishers will manage to do so either.

Is it really surprising in the light of these various factors that, for the same quality of work, the prices offered by the new generation of desktop publishers are remarkably close to those offered by their 'traditional' competitors. At the end of the day it may well be that the relative stagnation of the cost of text assembly over the last decade has been more the result of over-capacity, cut-throat price competition and reductions in the quality of products and services, than of falling equipment costs and rising user-friendliness. For hard and software only accounts for a small proportion of total investment and running costs. The fall in the price of machines is at least partly offset by the costs of keeping abreast of technical developments, training, and the maintainance of a sound customer base (to mention only the most obvious 'hidden' investment costs).

It is all too easy to imagine that radical technological change will inevitably have a major impact on the nature of typographical work. However, typography would appear to be remarkably resistant to technical revolutions. The adoption of direct inputting in the seventies, for example, did not reduce the need for typographical skills in text and page assembly. Rather it displaced the intervention of the specialist – either upstream towards the preparation stage, or downstream towards the page make-up stage. It was a simple case of taylorization, the extension of principles of labour organization known and practised in composing rooms since the fifteenth century. Similarly, WYSIWYG working did not eliminate the need for skills in spelling or grammar or the need to master long-established rules governing typographical practice, æsthetics and legibility. On the contrary, it is more urgent than ever to teach these skills to a much wider section of the population, if only because, compared with traditional compositors, desktop publishers work without a safety net. With copy preparation and proofreading increasingly regarded by many as an expensive luxury, there is no longer anybody to pick up the pieces behind 'text originators' who are usually more interested in the content of their productions than in their form.

It would, however, be absurd to argue that technological change is irrelevant to typography. It is still necessary to distinguish among the various techniques used in typographical production, if only because a full mastery of the production process depends on a knowledge of the specific characteristics of each process. But it is essential not to confuse the tool with the activity. No matter how sophisticated, accessible or ergonomic the tool, the work that it can turn out is ultimately limited by the skill of its user. For the moment at least, the computer still cannot reconcile the demands of production with the needs of the reader or resolve the myriad æsthetic questions raised by even the simplest printed product.

The micro-computer and the laser printer are tools for manipulating and reproducing texts. As such they change neither the nature of the raw material (a string of alphanumerical characters, spaces and punctuation marks which has to be structured according to the constraints imposed by the intended function of the text and conditions under which it will be used), nor the nature of the finished product (whose characteristics have to correspond to its intended use). The composition of type will continue to be marked by considerable specialization because of the nature of its raw material and of its finished products.

Tomorrow's typographers

Specialization, however, implies a differentiation of skills. And to come back to the question of comparisons between desktop publishing and traditional techniques, it is clear that, in labour terms, they involve quite different skills: that of the compositor (based on a recognized training and economically negotiable); and that of the majority of desktop publishers working within non print-related firms or administrations (usually ill-paid and insufficiently recognized). The true professional identity of a great number of new typographical workers is hidden by a job description which often has little or nothing to do with their actual daily activities.

However, desktop publishers are not the first professional category to have gone through this almost classic stage of non-recognition before going on to claim a recognized place within the labour market. The typographical designer, for example, was the result of the progressive separation of conception and execution which had been taking place over a long period. But it was several decades before typographical design was recognized as a distinct discipline within the graphic industries.

The gradual process by which the latest wave of new typographers might define its identity within the workforce is not hard to imagine. It starts with the appearance of commercial trade fairs organized by manufacturers eager to stabilize and expand a new equipment market (desktop publishing in this case). Such trade fairs soon provide the occasion for conferences aimed at providing a better understanding of the problems thrown up by the new techniques and their products. User groups soon follow, intended to provide mutual aid in the face of technical problems, and eventually becoming a forum for the exchange of ideas and experiences. The emergence of professional organizations is encouraged by a parallel movement in the workplace. Those employees who are most involved in using the new techniques begin to build up a professional identity within their organization, if only because in looking for ways to develop their own personal skills they discover the diversity of typography (and perhaps even some of the complex reasons which lie behind it). After months of constantly reinventing the wheel in order to get the most out of their Mac, they realize why compositors have tenaciously clung to a collective know-how accumulated over five centuries. Thus tiny typographical strongholds begin to appear, reinforced by an additional budget increase here and the occasional redefinition of a job description there. In the end, having thrown the compositor out the front door, the typographical specialist has crept back in the back!

Is it simply nostalgia, then, to imagine that all the fracas created by the Macintosh will one day be remembered simply as a another colourful episode in the long and continuing history of typography? Is it pure sour grapes on the part of a printer brought up with second generation phototypesetting dinosaurs to suggest that in those realms of activity in which typographical products and services are bought and sold for hard cash the notion of desktop publishing has no future in the long term? For although desktop publishing has passed into current vocabulary and is used today by more people than ever even knew of the existence of phototypesetting in the past, it is much less sure that its meaning has found its definitive form. For the moment it symbolizes a New Deal in typography and the end of the monopoly traditionally exerted by a handful of machine manufacturers within the printing industry. However, as it is used today, the term leads to a host of confusions. Firstly, it royally ignores any distinction between typographical production as a commercial and industrial activity, and as a means of interpersonal communication. No one really objects to the inevitable imperfections found in personal correspondence or in the welter of ephemeral working documents which oils the wheels of commerce, industry and government at all levels. (Just as nobody worried when it was hand- or typewritten.) However, these same imperfections become suddenly intolerable as soon as the products involved become the object of a commercial transaction. Secondly, this wonderfully universal term is so intimately linked with a particular technology (a particular make of computer even) that one might legitimately wonder what will happen when the famous Fourth Wave has passed and everyone is using standard micro-computers and workstations for typographical applications? Can desktop publishing hope to maintain a separate identity within a sector which will be differentiated, not by a cleavage between the new and the old, but by a complex hierarchy based on quality and precision, stretching from informal personal production to indus-trial production for an increasingly demanding market.

Each innovation in the typographic field incorporates a little bit more of the typographer's know-how. Each new machine takes automation a step further. But the pool of typographical know-ledge is not limited. It too is constantly expanding, keeping one step ahead of the machines. Ideas which were prohibitively expen-sive to carry out yesterday become commonplace and are integ-rated within the corpus of typographical know-how. Each new tool increases the typographers' power – assuming that the typo-graphers know how to use it and to what end. Does it matter in the end whether they work in a design studio, in an office, or at home rather than in a composing room? For as in botany, so in typography, 'That which we call a rose by any other name would smell as sweet'!

PART 5

RESEARCH AND THE PERCEPTION OF TYPE

Through the eyes of a child – perception and type design

ROSEMARY SASSOON LETTERFORM CONSULTANT AND RESEARCHER, 34 WITCHES LANE, SEVENOAKS, KENT. UK TN13 2AX

Little thought has ever been given to designing specific typefaces for those learning to read. No one considered that children might perceive letterforms in a different way. Research showed children to be quite capable of making the necessary discriminations. The resulting typefaces bridge the gap between reading and writing. with implications for computer generated letters and other issues not necessarily confined to education.

The visual analysis of pages of text

ROGER WATT PROFESSOR OF PSYCHOLOGY, UNIVERSITY OF STIRLING, SCOTLAND. FK9 4LA

The moment is opportune for an examination of just what the visual effects of the various possible word and line spacings are. In this paper I describe a little of visual perception, a little of typography and some formal experiments into the relationship between the two.

ROSEMARY SASSOON

Through the eyes of a child – Perception and type design

One of the main principles of typography has always been to ensure the suitability of the typeface for a particular purpose. It is somewhat astonishing, therefore, that little thought has ever been given to designing specific typefaces for those learning to read. Typographic researchers, Ovink (1935) above all others, have stressed the atmosphere values of types and how this might affect the reader. Zachrisson (1967) pointed out that, 'Good typography tries to make the message as legible and accessible as possible. Thus the relation between the reader and the image is the function, whose efficiency is to be judged. Typography will consequently have to be regarded as a *psychological* problem.' The decision about letterforms, however, has always been taken by adults for children. Such decisions are often made by educationists without specialist knowledge of letterforms, or by designers whose criteria for making a page attractive may not be in the children's best interest. It seems that no one has considered that young children might perceive letterforms in a different way to adults and therefore have different requirements. Worse still, no one seemed to think it important enough to ask children for their views.

Watts and Nisbet (1974) noted 'No study of the legibility of typefaces which uses children as subjects has been found. The inference made by many researchers regarding the legibility of different typefaces for use in children's books has been based on:

1   legibility studies carried out with adults or older children
2   their idea of what is involved in the process of learning to read
3   the relation of reading and writing skills. (This last consideration is not strictly a matter of legibility, although it

may influence a teacher's opinion of what constitutes a 'legible' typeface.)

As far as can be established nothing has been done actively with children since then. Raban (1984) used a questionnaire to ask teachers about their views on typefaces. This revealed that when asked to choose between serifed or sans serif typefaces there was a clear indication that a sans serif typeface was preferred by two-thirds of the teachers for books through the infant stage. However, when questioned further about their priorities for typefaces under the rather widely interpreted heading of 'Styles of Print', the picture was somewhat more revealing.

Styles of print in books (in rank order of mention) (n=150)

1	Didn't matter after seven years of age	54%
2	Print should match handwriting	39%
3	Modified a and g	14%
4	Size of print	11%
5	Letter shapes should be simple	10%
6	Didn't matter at all	5%
7	Consistency	
	Spacing important	2%
8	Sans serif typeface	
	good story mattered more	1%

The meagre 2% who considered spacing important even when coupled with the term 'consistent' illustrates how little those teachers' priorities reflected children's real needs.

Yule (1988) expressed refreshing and informed views on the subject in an aptly named paper, 'The Design of Print for Children: Sales Appeal and User Appeal'. She also had to report that, apart from Watts and Nisbet, it is difficult to find any research about print for learners. I particularly like her remark that 'There has been a trend for some aspects of lettering and layout to be designed for sales appeal rather than user appeal. The goal of sales appeal is often for print that is meant to be looked at rather than read'. She also pointed out that 'The current fashion for very closely spaced words and letters produces blocks and lines of print which have a pleasing overall pattern when glanced at. The

complex pattern is not designed to be looked at closely – the effect
is like an intricate all-over carpet pattern.'

My views – for what they are worth

Leaving research aside and using only common-sense observations,
many of the features of typefaces that are fashionable today are
entirely adult-orientated, suited admirably to the fluent reader. The
combination of fashion and the desire to pack as many lines as
possible onto a page, has resulted in decreased ascenders and
descenders. This tendency eventually erodes the shape of a word as
well as the actual identity of individual letters.

I have been involved in letterforms all my working life, but until
recently I have not been closely involved in type design. After a
decade's work in handwriting problems, I was well aware of the
injustice of the imposition of various idiosyncratic handwriting
models on young children, and the harm that could be done by
not considering this from the writer's point of view. Such views
are reported in Sassoon (1983, 1990 etc.). When it was brought to
my notice that similar attitudes in the area of typographic design
and layout might affect children's reading performance, then it
seemed that this deserved investigation. It all started when I was
visiting a remedial centre to see a child with handwriting
problems. The teacher in charge approached me, and I can still
remember her exact words. She said '*You know all kinds of odd
things*, can you tell me why my pupils with learning difficulties can
read one page and not the next, although the vocabulary is at the
same level?' A quick glance at the pages of a popular reading
scheme revealed that the one causing problems was the first to be
justified. This term meant nothing to the teacher, so it had to be
explained to her.

Justified or unjustified text

Hartley and Burnhill (1973) reported on comparisons between
justified and unjustified text. Justifying is described by them as
follows: 'If the reader examines any textbook he will most
probably observe that the right-hand margin of the text is straight:
that the lines of type are forced – by variable word spacing and the
use of hyphens – into what printers call "justified" text. An
alternative strategy to this is to provide equal spacing between the

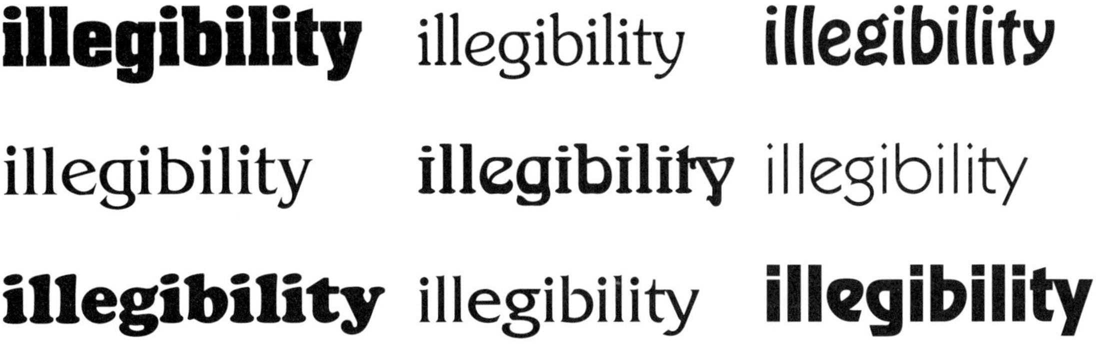

illegibility *illegibility* **illegibility**

illegibility **illegibility** illegibility

illegibility illegibility **illegibility**

Figure 1
A selection of modern typefaces – and there are many worse – showing some awkward characters and spacing.

words and consequently to produce line lengths that are irregular.' They continue, 'There is little apart from tradition to justify justified text . . . Justifiying the text causes unco-ordinated word spaces whereas unjustified text is the result of coordinating the sign system.'

Their conclusions tended to favour unjustified text but they included a wise proviso. 'Typography is remarkable for its numbers of variables – all of which interact – i.e. size and style of type, spacing between words and lines, line length etc. Systematic research, varying one or two features at a time, ignores this complexity.' The references to further research into justification quoted in Hartley and Burnhill, and later in Watts and Nesbitt, were all confined to work with adult readers. (See also James Hartley's chapter in this volume.) The last word should perhaps come from Eric Gill (1931), taken from his *Essay on Typography*: 'A book is primarily a thing to be read, and the merely neat appearance of a page of type of which all the lines are equal in length is a thing of no very great value.' He also said about the equality of line length that it 'can be obtained in a page of 10-12 word lines only by the sacrifice of more important things.'

To a designer unfamiliar with or unimpressed by Gill's argument, a justified page may represent a pleasingly neat appearance but from the children's point of view two disadvantages are apparent. To children with problems, justification could produce a menacing rectangle of text without any helpful clues to guide them in their reading. Justification can also play havoc with spacing on a page of fairly large type where there are only a few words (usually fewer than Gill's 10-12) to a line. Two short words may end up so close together that they appear to be one. This would confuse those children who depend on recognizing the word shape.

The project

The word research is used to describe anything from a primary school-child's project to scientific studies. I tend to use this word cautiously and do not wish to present the following project in too serious a manner. This does not mean that I consider the findings unimportant, rather to the contrary. Meaningful conclusions can be retrieved from relatively simple but informed and carefully planned surveys, particularly when they are carried out in real-life situations. Too many generalizations should not be claimed from such findings; however, as in this case, vital information can sometimes be extracted.

The project that led to the design of a family of child-orientated typefaces started in relatively low key manner. It was initially concerned with spacing rather than with the letterforms themselves. There was no precedent for testing children on their perception either of spacing or of the different elements of letters. Almost everyone that I discussed this with considered this task to be beyond the capabilities of young children. No funding was sought, and its success was dependent on the cooperation of hardworking teachers. The teachers involved had no particular typographic knowledge. It was perhaps better that they should know as little as possible in case their own views affected their judgement. It was essential, however, that they should have detailed knowledge of individual pupils' reading capacity. This project was offered to several special needs teachers in various parts of Great Britain. An exact method of testing was not specified. This was because all the work would have to be undertaken during professional working hours. It is not surprising that only one teacher was able to produce a worthwhile study, as that took her over a year to produce.

The task

The text of the original problem page was re-set in five different spacings through the generosity of the Monotype Corporation. The spacings that were selected were:

1 Justified: Solid setting

2 Justified: 18 point on 30 point body. Increased word spacing.
3 Unjustified: 18 point on 30 point body. Increased word space doubled before each new sentence.
4 Unjustified: 18 point on 30 point body. Double word spacing
5 Unjustified: 18 point on 30 point body. Double word spacing, new sentence new line.

It was then that a choice of typefaces had to be made. With little guidance from previous research it could be called arbitrary. In the field of learning difficulties, however, such matters were already under discussion in an informal way. The choice was, of course, confined to existing typefaces and between serifed and sans serif letters, either upright or slanted. Times Roman, the establishment's usual recommendation, was an obvious choice. Times Italic was included as some people involved with children with reading problems were already recommending it. Helvetica (with simplified a and g) was chosen because of its popularity with educational publishers, and my personal inclusion was a slanting sans serif typeface. In this way twenty variables were available.

The method
The teacher used one hundred children. Half of them were pupils with special needs whose ages ranged from eight to thirteen years. The other fifty were eight-year-old children in mainstream education. The first group were shown each of the four typefaces set solid and asked to choose the one that they preferred. Whether this was the best method or not, it was the one chosen by the teacher who thought that sixteen variables would be too much for the children with problems. They were then exposed to the four different spacings in their chosen typeface and asked which they preferred for reading. The fifty eight-year-olds were given a more difficult task. They were not shown the typefaces set solid, but were exposed to the other sixteen variables. They were then tested individually to see which they liked best and which they found easiest to read. These proved not always to be the same.

Findings
Let me start by quoting the valiant teacher, Dorothy Ibbotson from Doncaster. 'Children who were very poor readers preferred

He was right out of the water and away from the waves and he lay still. He rolled on to his back, and lay very still. He lay there for a long time. He blew and puffed, and lay there on the sand. And as he lay there, the wind blew more softly and the clouds began to blow away. There was a little blue sky. The sun began to shine a little.

He was right out of the water and away from the waves and he lay still. He rolled on to his back, and lay very still. He lay there for a long time. He blew and puffed, and lay there on the sand. And as he lay there, the wind blew more softly and the clouds began to blow away. There was a little blue sky. The sun began to shine a little.

He was right out of the water and away from the waves and he lay still. He rolled on to his back, and lay very still. He lay there for a long time. He blew and puffed, and lay there on the sand. And as he lay there, the wind blew more softly and the clouds began to blow away. There was a little blue sky. The sun began to shine a little.

Figure 2
Three of the traditional typefaces used to test children's preferences.

Fig 2a
The fourth and most favoured typeface. These four examples were set unjustified, 18pt. on 30 pt. body. Increased word space doubled before each new sentence.

He was right out of the water and away from the waves and he lay still. He rolled on to his back, and lay very still. He lay there for a long time. He blew and puffed, and lay there on the sand. And as he lay there, the wind blew more softly and the clouds began to blow away. There was a little blue sky. The sun began to shine a little.

wide spacing and plain print (*slanted sans serif*). More intelligent children and better readers enjoyed reading script (*Times italic*) and liked narrow spacing.' The italics are my own interpretations after talking to the teacher.

The part of the study concerning spacing, reinforces my own view about matters as personal and variable as handwriting or perception of letterforms. Presenting the findings as an average or norm is not always the most useful way to describe them. In this case, the teacher's astute observations and the children's comments were invaluable in building up a picture of how, even within this small sample, children at different levels of reading had different

Figure 3
The same text set in Sassoon Primary.

He was right out of the water and away from the waves and he lay still. He rolled on to his back, and lay very still. He lay there for a long time. He blew and puffed, and lay there on the sand. And as he lay there, the wind blew more softly and the clouds began to blow away. There was a little blue sky. The sun began to shine a little.

requirements for spacing. In particular, the 'new sentence new line' favoured by the readers with the lowest level of reading capacity positively annoyed more fluent eight-year-olds.

The findings on preference for typefaces showed that children are quite capable of making the necessary discriminations. The teacher reported 'All were very interested in the project, enjoyed talking about the print and were very firm and verbose about their opinions.' This interest and perceptive capability has been confirmed by subsequent, more detailed work with even younger children. This brings to mind two anecdotes concerning children's perceptions of type.

My colleague Briem, whose chapter in this volume on layout proclaims his lifelong interest in letterforms, remembers, at about the age of seven, throwing back a book that an unsuspecting relative had just given him because the bold sans serif typeface offended him. He still has the book to prove the point. Valerie Yule (1988) said that she had only kept one school reading book. 'It was not because of the stories, but because I liked the print so much.'

> There was once a poor woman who had two daughters, named Rose and Minnie. They lived in a small house near a wood.

Figure 4
A school book treasured because of its 'print', not its content. From an illustration in Yule (1988).

In the study described above, the letterform preferences were unexpected. The overall favourite was the slanted sans serif (36%), with Times Italic in second place (26%), Helvetica third (20%) and Times Roman least favoured at (18%). The children with learning difficulties showed the most marked preferences: 44% read best when using slanting sans serif, 28% with Times Italic, 18% with Helvetica. Only 10% chose Times Roman. This is not surprising, as the combination of pronounced serifs and fairly short descenders, in particular, affect the identity of certain letters.

How this information was used

It would not be true to say that the educational typefaces now called Sassoon Primary were based entirely on the evidence provided by this survey. Certain elements could be isolated from the survey, in particular the desirability of a slight slant. While designing the letterforms I had always to be aware that the children had had only adult features to choose from. My job was to build extra legibility and friendliness into the forms. Balancing the overall preference for sans serif with the comments about liking the 'kick-up' of Times Italic a new kind of letter evolved that cannot be described in typographic terms as either seriffed or sans serif.

Figure 5
This graph indicates the preferences for typefaces and spacing of fifty remedial children, and fifty eight-year olds in mainstream education.

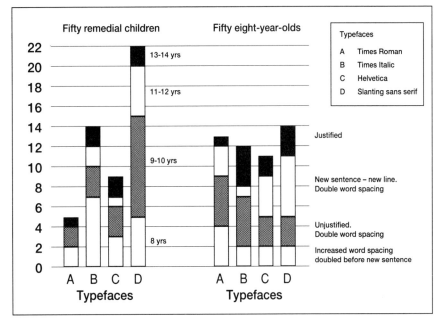

If this typeface had to be described by ATypI's 'parameters of originality' it might upset their neat categorization. The child-orientated letters have sans serif terminals for the ascending strokes, to maximize clarity along the top of the line of text. However, letters that terminate on the baseline do not have anything that could be termed a serif. It is more a flowing 'kick up'. This 'exit stroke' to use a handwriting term, has two functions: to ensure clear letter spacing while at the same time clumping the letters of each word together along the baseline into a more cohesive shape. The length of the ascenders and descenders was increased, bearing in mind the uses of such a typeface and the need to allow for moderately close line spacing. The smooth arches were designed to accentuate the movement, and particular care was taken to simplify the counters. As well as improving legibility these features added a juvenile and friendly atmosphere to the letterforms.

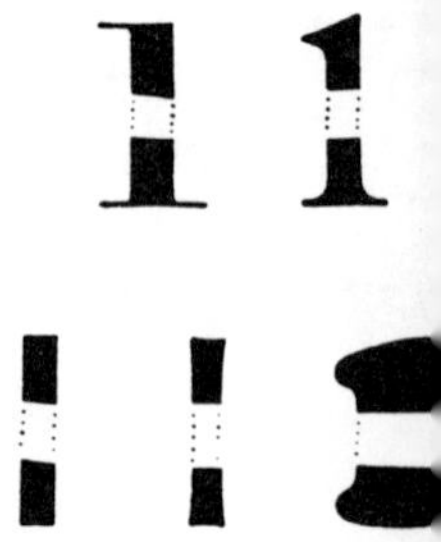

Bridging the gap between reading and writing

The typeface was researched and designed to be read, but the elements that children chose, and therefore formed the basis of my design, included many of the features of handwriting. There is little historical precedent for the two sets of letters to be identical.

The teachers in Raban's survey reported that it was desirable to have identical letters for reading and writing. This comment is likely to have a different interpretation from that stated by Schonell and Goodacre (1971) that; 'The type should resemble as nearly as possible the print script that the child is acquainted with in his writing. This can be achieved by 24 point Gill Sans type'. By 1984 the teachers were more likely to be looking at it from the other angle. They were probably trying to justify the use of print script as a handwriting model by claiming that it was a good idea to write the same letters as those that appear in reading books – under the mistaken impression that only sans serif typefaces are used in children's books.

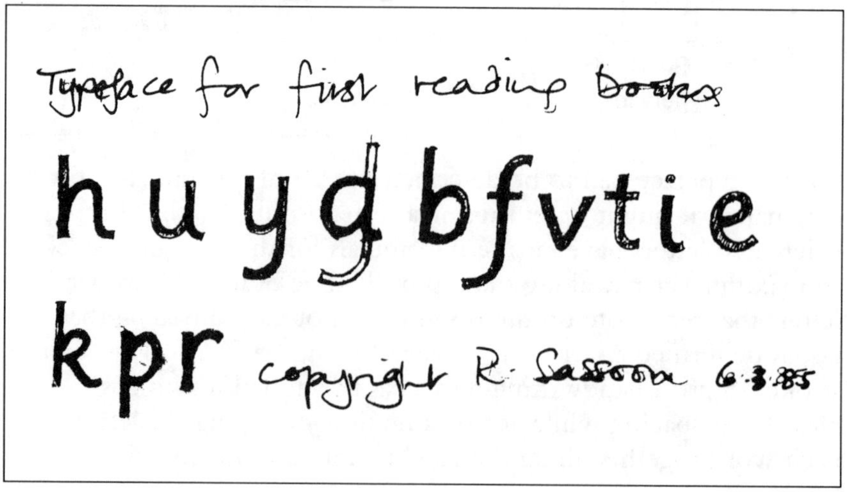

Figure 6
Terminals of letters illustrated in ATypI's 'Parameters of Originality' 1984.

Figure 7
Little has been altered since my first scribbled sketch for Sassoon Primary Type in 1985.

Both of these arguments can now be refuted – the reading argument here in this article, and the one about writing in Sassoon (1990). It is now increasingly accepted that, from school entry, children should be exposed to handwriting models that have baseline exits built into the letters. This promotes a more flowing movement and an easier progression to a joined hand.

Yule (1988) had some useful comments to make from the perceptual angle: 'The assumption has been that unless print for children's early reading and writing is identical, the children will be confused – again on the analogy with an optical scanner. This is what you would expect for a computer brain. However, people are different. One of the earliest features of human learning is its capacity for broad-band categorization and generalisation.' I would agree with Valerie Yule that there is no proof at all to support the proposition that most children find it difficult to discriminate between simple written and printed forms, even forms of the letters 'g' and 'a'. On the contrary, in real-life situations, our children are, from an early age, bombarded by television graphics and other advertising. Apart from those with severe perceptual problems, children appear to assimilate the different forms quite happily. This seems to be an adult perception of a possible problem more than a child's – but it is a good subject for a research project if anyone is interested.

In the meantime, a new factor has emerged. In answer to a publisher's investigation into attitudes to the new typeface, one teacher went further than surveying it for reading purposes. She volunteered, 'I pursued a separate issue with my question "Would you like to write like this?" The children replied enviously that they certainly would. They were obviously impressed with the *style of print* (my italics) and I as a teacher saw tremendous advantages in developing a typeface that could link with a handwriting scheme.' There would be advantages for a publisher too, as a handwriting-like typeface would bypass the extremely expensive business of hiring a 'scribe' to produce all the necessary copybooks. When the inevitable proposal turned up I could not have prevented it, even if I had wanted to. I am not particularly in favour of commercial handwriting schemes and had no intention of producing one myself, but by then anyone could buy the postscript version of Sassoon Primary Type, install it on their

Figure 8
Written and printed letterforms side by side. From The Adelaide First Primer, South Australia, 1897.

computer and go straight ahead – but were these letters right for a handwriting model? They had a certain amount of movement built into them so perhaps it was only a matter of increasing the ascenders and descenders – or was it? Not only did this project become, from that moment, market-led, but the new uses meant a completely new and flexible attitude to the set of letters. There was a whole new set of problems too.

The case for alternative letters

A nine-year-old in one of the early surveys made an astute comment: 'Some letters are difficult to copy but easier to read'. There was, anyhow, a strong case for including certain alternative letters, both within the two usages and between them. With modern technology there is no reason why alternatives should not be provided. Given a choice, whoever is specifying the letterforms might start to think of the end user – and that would benefit all our children. A few are detailed below.

The letter 'k'

There has long been controversy in handwriting circles about the comparative merits of a closed, continuously written one or an open spiky one. There are two schools of thought – those who consider that each letter (except 'x' 't' and 'f') should be written without a penlift, and those who think that the continuous 'k' looks like a capital 'R'. Moreover, they think the spiky open k is easier for children to write. There was an obvious need for both to be available for teaching handwriting. For general typographic purposes the open 'k' would usually be preferable It retains its clarity even when very small.

The letter 'q'

A plain one looks like a reversed 'p', and is seldom written that way for children to copy; but one with a 'tail' that accentuates the identity might not work well typographically. It introduces an unfamiliar and unwelcome weight along the line of descending strokes.

The letter 'f'

The long 'f' is my choice for handwriting. I have always thought it

Figure 9
Some of the alternative letters developed for the family of typefaces

best to teach, from the start, the form that will be needed in a joined handwriting. The descending one works quite well typographically and there are precedents in italic forms. In child-orientated terms, the longer form enhances the word shape. However, it seemed prudent to provide the alternative short form for either writing or printing.

Capitals needed thought too. Alternative forms for I and J were requested, with bar serifs. They were thought to be more easily identifiable for young children specially in projects for children with special needs and those learning English as a second language. An alternative 'G' was added that was closer to a handwritten form. All these alternatives were added to updated sets, along with child-orientated numerals. Some of the forms might fill traditional typographers with horror, but that is not the point. There was a perceived need for them by specialist publishers.

Market-led innovations

An upright typeface both for reading and writing was yet another market-led departure. This is quite a simple alteration to make using the original Ikarus data. By now the whole project was getting further and further away from its relatively researched beginnings, and more was to come. A joined version was a challenge that could not be resisted – but it brought with it considerable complications. These have not yet all been solved in a satisfactory way. More than any previous venture, the joined letters mark the point where the priorities for reading and writing differ.

The joined version for teaching handwriting needed handwriting, not typographic ligatures. It needed to show how letters joined, not only give a cursive appearance. Half a dozen joins to the letter 'e' or to and from 's' were needed, for example, making the keying in of continuous text rather tedious. There was also a major ideological problem for me. I believe that the hand needs a rest as it progresses along the line, and recommend penlifts every few letters. This is not necessarily in any particular mathematical sequence. The need for a penlift is governed partly by how many complex movements have had to be made in any series of letters. The frequency of penlifts is also likely to vary with individual size, speed and style of writing and the handiness of the

for

the

men

and

Figure 10
The cursive letters were designed to show hand-written letters join.

writer. My convictions put me in no mood to provide anyone
with the means of printing out long lines of continuous cursive to
torture the children who might have to copy them. Then there is
the matter of the need for alternative letterforms for such letters as
's','f', and 't' when they are joined. These alternative joins are easy
to design but impossible to program in such a way that they would
suit individual writers. So far I have limited the use of the joined
handwriting fount to pairs of joined letters. These can show how
to join, and can be used for demonstrating various alternatives to
encourage experimentation.

Visually these 'handwriting' joins disrupt the midline in particular
and, in doing so, they interfere with the smooth scanning of text.
From the typographic angle any looped ascenders or descenders
that would be practical (or, in this case, dare I say, aesthetic) to
write would be far too long for any reasonable line-spacing. A
simplified cursive-looking typeface, perhaps for use in advertising
is now possible, but even that would be unlikely to be practical for
long texts.

Learning from various usages of the typefaces

It has been interesting to see how various independent designers
have reacted to the special advantages of these new letterforms.
Here are three examples.

Mirror image discrimination
One of the criticisms of simplified sans serif letters has been that
they offer no clues to those who confuse letters that are mirror

Figure 11
'Pick the odd one out'
reads the caption to this
illustration in Hodder
and Stoughton's
'Writing and Spelling. A
good use of the typeface
to help discriminate
between the letters 'b'
and 'd'.

images of each other. As Yule (1988) says, 'There is much less difficulty for "beginning" readers if their first introduction to p-d-b-q those letter shapes are similar to "adult" print. Then there are differences in weighting, and the form and position of serifs.' A weighted version is still to come but one designer was quick to note the advantages of the difference between the 'b' and the 'd'. He used Sassoon Primary when this discrimination was being stressed but still clung to good old Helvetica in other places on the same page.

Copying under printed text
Up to now we have been discussing two different categories of letters: those that you read and those that you write. But there is an intermediate category. With the change in teaching methods, more and more children work from either commercial or school-produced worksheets. This means that children spend a fair amount of time copying or writing under printed text. Few children would be confused by the difference in letterforms, but the spacing is a different matter. Take a look at some worksheets and notice how closely the letters and words are spaced. There is seldom enough room for children to copy underneath in their own handwriting. The spacing should be more realistic if the recommendations that come with the new typeface are followed. Designers have also been quick to realize that children can now copy under printed text that looks more friendly and inviting.

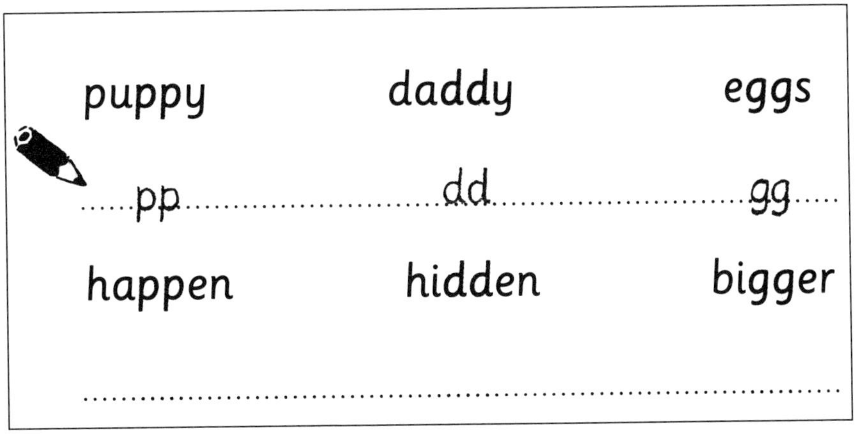

Figure 12
The exit strokes that space the typeface also allow more room for children to copy underneath printed words. From Linguaphone Children's English.

puppy   daddy   eggs

.....pp.................................dd..................................gg.....

happen   hidden   bigger

41

Accentuating informality

An early use of the typeface was for a maths project. The publisher used the new typeface to bring informality to a rather rigid project and to make it as appealing as possible. The use of the typefaces in balloons in a comic strip format also makes good use of the informality without losing legibility

Opportunities for usage in education

There are no precedents for such flexible usage of typefaces, if that is even the right name for these sets of letters. There are still considerable problems to overcome. The question arises, should there now be separate founts recommended for reading and for

Figure 13
The informality of the typefaces means that they work well in a comic-strip format. From New Horizons Science 5-16. Cambridge University Press.

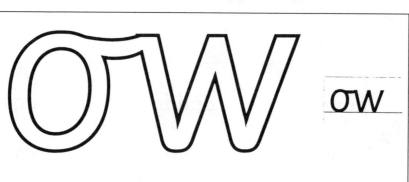

Figure 14
The joined typeface in outline, used to teach young children to track joins between pairs of letters. From Ginns Handwriting.

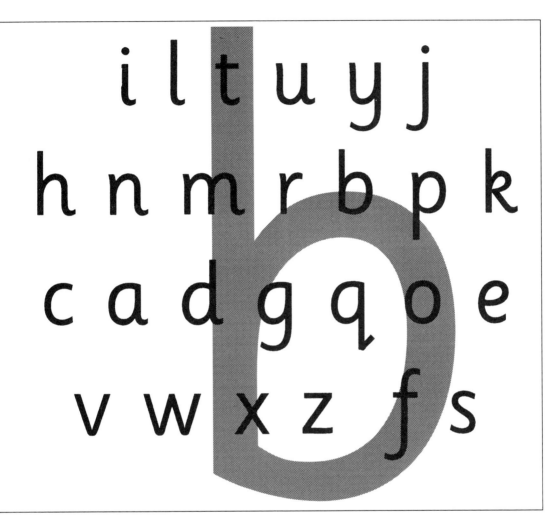

Figure 15
Letter families for handwriting (even more effective in colour) or large letters for a classroom frieze are examples of pupil material that can easily be produced by teachers on the school computer.

writing? How much does the way you write affect the way you are able to decipher letters with ease, especially joined ones? Could the use of a joined-up typeface help young writers to understand the joins in their own handwriting – or to decipher adult handwriting?

An ever-increasing number of books for young children are now using one or other of these typefaces. This is the result of the enthusiastic response from publishers and others. As these new letters become more familiar to young children maybe they will lead to progessive improvement in reading capacity.

Now individual schools, districts, counties or even countries can produce on their own computers consistent reading, spelling and writing materials for use with young children. There could be many incidental advantages in the future. One might be that instead of having to rely on the inflexible and often inappropriate commercial work-sheets, teachers could produce their own pupil material. They could combine the teaching of these three subjects as they wished. It might be time-consuming in the first year, but the material, once used, could then be stored. It could be retrieved the next year and improved if necessary. In a relatively short period of time, teachers could have their own tried and tested pupil material ideally suited to their particular needs.

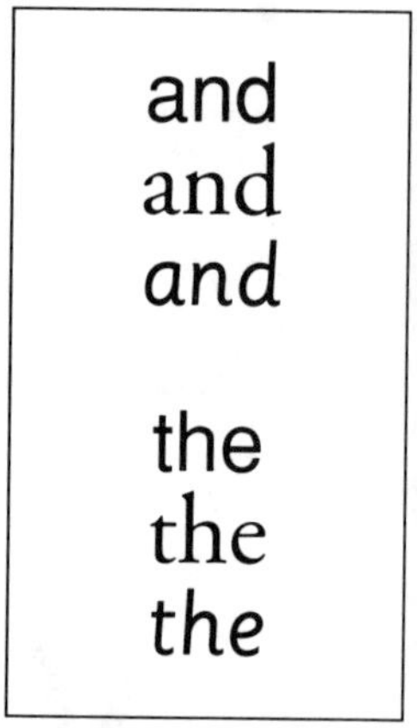

What further surveys have been done
Before pioneering the use of the new typeface several publishers carried out their own investigations. No great weight can be given to such surveys, though luckily they must have influenced the brave publishers who took the risk of trying something new. Teachers reported that the children read the passages with greater ease and fluency than expected or 'Better still there was a high degree of reading with expression'. Comments such as that of a six-year-old – 'I like the writing, I like the curly "*f*", or "I loved *puffed*", or "I loved *softly*" (words in the text) from another school's report, showed that children noticed details. Both sets of reactions might have been accounted for by the novelty of the children having been asked for their opinions.

A more systematic enquiry was carried out by a young Norwegian designer, Siri Askildsen, first at an undergraduate level, then a second stage during post-graduate studies. Her work was sponsored by an international company involved in educational toys and equipment. The aim was to investigate the effects of styles of typefaces and illustration on how children assimilate instructional text. Her techniques included using 'bingo'-like games to see how quickly and accurately young children could discriminate between details of typefaces. This was followed by single-word tests to compare these new typefaces with traditional ones. In this way she not only tested the actual letterforms but made some interesting headway into discovering the number of variables that it was possible for children of five years and upwards

Figure 16
The words 'and' and 'the' printed in different typefaces were used in a 'bingo-like' game to see how easily young children could perceive the difference in detail.

to deal with. In her later work a check was made to ensure that it was not just novelty that attracted the children to a new typeface. Three sizes of each typeface were used and the same question about which was easiest to read was asked. More children chose the Sassoon Primary Typeface as the size decreased. This can be explained by the increased need for legibility at a reduced size. In addition, many of those who chose Helvetica did so because they said that they read it best because they were used to it. Such comments are valuable in assessing the value of the original survey too, but much more methodical work remains to be done before anything can be said to be proven.

There was a limit to young children's capacity for discrimination. We wanted to investigate how the use of a friendly child-orientated typeface might alter the atmosphere of a page. It is easy enough to demonstrate this by using overlays. This can change the mood of the whole page. When this technique was tried out with young children, it was found that they had considerable difficulty even with terminology for describing the different atmospheres. This is hardly surprising, but it meant that this aspect of the survey could not be pursued. It remains yet another fascinating subject to research 'one day'.

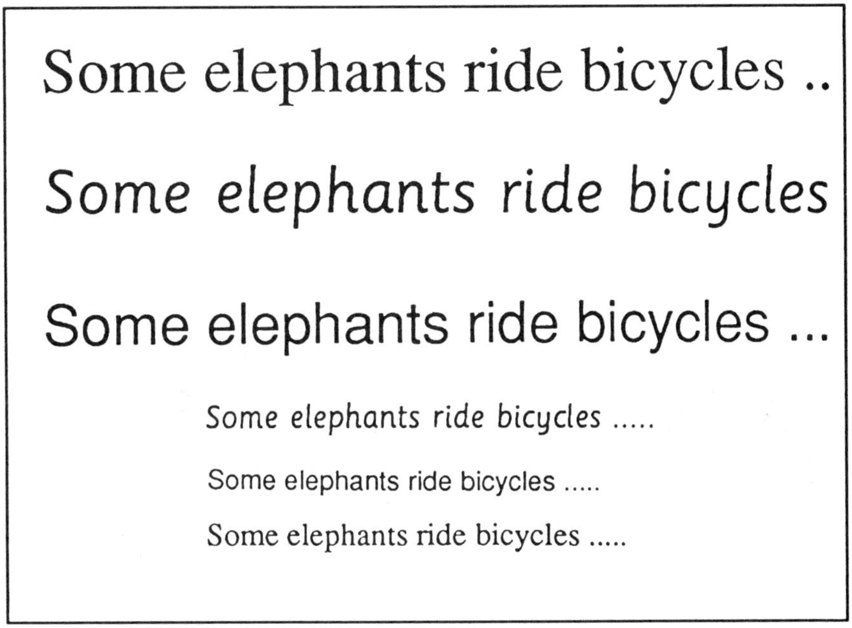

Figure 17
At smaller sizes more children chose Sassoon Primary because of its legible features.

Some elephants ride bicycles ..

Some elephants ride bicycles

Some elephants ride bicycles ...

Some elephants ride bicycles .....

Some elephants ride bicycles .....

Some elephants ride bicycles .....

Figure 18
Altering the typeface
can alter the atmosphere
of the page. This is not
easy to judge from these
reduced illustrations.
Children found it hard
to describe such
differences.

Now, as national and more localized bodies pursue their
enquiries into uses of this family of typefaces, both in mainstream
education and in special needs, we are all in the same situation:
working on the edge of knowledge. We are in an ever-changing
environment, and there is nothing to make real comparisons with.
I would welcome parallel research and other child-orientated
typefaces, but doubt if others are likely to be forthcoming in the
present economic condition. The original research, and the type-
design, were both time-consuming and expensive.

Implications for computers in education

The purpose of this article is not only to report on this particular
project but to bring to everyone's attention the need to consider
the requirements of different classes of readers, and also to
highlight the implications for computer-generated letters in
education in general. While earnest deliberations no doubt take
place before investment is made in new hardware, from what I see,
even in specialist schools, little thought seems to be given to the
actual letterforms produced by the latest, most expensive printer.
Once more Yule (1988) had something relevant to say:
'Mechanical factors in print design can also operate against
readability by children. This includes the desk-top printers' spacing
which produce letter spacing where wide letters looked crammed
and narrow letters isolated.'

No discussion about type is complete without the views of
Hermann Zapf (1987). He wrote the following in a book about
David Kindersley's Workshop: 'We should not wonder today that
so many people nowadays – particularly young people – don't like
to read. The presentation in printed texts, and even more on TV or
personal computer screens, ignores completely the rules of
legibility. One of the rules is that letters should be picked up
quickly and accurately. Because this often does not happen, in the
end pictures are preferred. Today's fashion for tight spacing is one
of the problems. Too narrow spacing between characters taken to
the extreme slows down the speed of reading. Computer
generated letters can seldom be read comfortably; apart from the
poor design of the letterforms themselves the distances between
letters are uneven.'

Not long ago I visited a school for the blind, which actually had

Winter came. The trees were bare.
Snow lay on the ground.
Hungry animals were out hunting.
It was hard to find food.
But the dormouse slept safely in his
warm nest.

a large proportion of partially-sighted pupils, in the hope of investigating the special needs of that unusual and very variable group of children. The attitude of the establishment was that bold sans serif letters were precisely suited to all their children's needs. I accepted the verdict meekly then (I would not necessarily do so now after a few more experiments of my own) and took up an invitation to see the resource department that produced all their reading matter. The form of sans serif that was installed was

Figure 19
A child-orientated page aimed at 5–6 year-olds, that uses slightly wider word spacing than used in the research project. From New Horizons Science 5–16. Cambridge University Press.

appallingly spaced. The fact that the print was much larger than usual made matters worse. Even with normal vision it was often impossible to see where one word was supposed to end and the next began. Wherever the letter 'r' occurred a space equivalent to a word space followed. An 'm', however, had been allotted the same space as an 'n', 'mm' was a disaster. A few adjustments would have made all the difference, but no one wanted to listen.

Specialist teachers are now installing both upright and sloping versions of the new typefaces, normal weight and bold, into their 'laptops' and giving partially-sighted children a choice in addition to traditional sans serif. It is early days, but the results are not all negative. However a completely new set of readers deserves a completely new survey, with a completely open mind. Any volunteers?

Writing and printing are ambiguous words

Now to another different point. It is evident from various sources that both teachers and children are becoming confused over the difference between written and printed letters. The ambiguous terminology does not help. That one word 'writing' means different things to different people. In addition, for many years the word 'print' has referred to separate handwritten letters as well as to mechanically printed letters. Now however a more subtle factor has arisen. Computers are increasingly in use in the classroom, and perhaps the two sets of letters are becoming more closely interrelated. Are the barriers less evident as more and more children look to keyboards as a normal tool for communicating their thoughts?

At the same time, a more insidious problem needs looking into. Do we create words and record thoughts in the same way when using a computer as we do when writing by hand? Many adult writers of this transitional generation find the computer a 'cold' instrument for creative writing. Authors and poets can be heard saying that they express their feelings better by the more personal route, via the hand to the paper. On the other hand, writers of non-fiction and academic writers tend to welcome the organizational facility of the word-processor. Research is needed, but if we leave this particular investigation for too long, there will no longer be a 'handwriting-only' generation to study.

The pace of change in our schools is alarming. Are educationalists so sure that the computer is best and only way of recording, or are they succumbing to commercial pressures? They may be making the same mistake as many others have made in the five centuries since Gutenberg, believing that old adage – 'Handwriting is dead'. To write, to make your mark, is a basic human need. Moreover, adults who cannot present a consistent signature, or fill in a form, are non-persons in our society. They are dependent on someone else to conduct their business affairs.

Flexibile attitudes are needed to judge when a computer might be better than writing by hand. This would be most relevant when working with young children. One frequent method of combining handwriting and computer-generated letters in the classroom is to let children draft their ideas by hand and then transfer them at the final stage. In this way they obtain a professional-looking copy from the word processor. Then there is the opposite sequence of events where the organizational qualities of the computer are optimized in the early stages of recording and story-making, and the final copy is handwritten. By then, spelling as well as content would have been sorted out, both of them tasks that inhibit fluent handwriting.

Later on many pupils would profit from keyboards for note-taking. Those who recommend, them though, seldom take into account how long it takes a pupil to attain the necessary speed. Just one practical suggestion – why should not the outline of lessons be programmed into PCs with space built in for students to add their personal notes? The technology is there – but is there the understanding or the will to be flexible? Everything is in the melting pot, and all of us involved in letterforms, computers and education should start discussing these matters. Between ourselves, yes, but also with children. It is their attitudes that are important for the future and we must no longer ignore them as active participants in research.

Computers versus the human eye
We cannot depend on computers themselves to make the same judgements as the human eye – even when they have been carefully programmed to do so. An interesting analogy appears in the intricate work being done into machine recognition of letters.

Figure 20
Models used in Human
Recognition of Handprinted
Characters and Distance
Measurements, Suen (1986).

I have followed the research of Professor Suen of Concordia University, Montreal, among others, with interest over the years. Initially such work involved investigating the variability of written forms before a computer could be programmed to discriminate between the many variables – in numerals as well as alphabetic characters. Suen (1986) reports: 'While the distance measurements may produce characters that are more distinct in shapes, these characters may not be the same as those found most legible to humans (*adults aged* 18-30 *in this experiment*); indicating that selective information theory fails to explain human form perception. Human recognition of characters is based on a long learning process, wide experience and innate inheritance.' Can this perhaps be simplified to mean that legibility is in the eye of the perceiver? Recent work reported by Nadal and Suen (1991) suggests that 'when faced by complicated pairs for discrimination the machine seemed to use a more arbitrary scheme':

- It substitutes some samples that are unambiguous to humans
- It cannot differentiate between unambiguous and confusing patterns
- It often does not offer on the same possible class pairs as the humans when the sample is confusing.

The title of their paper is sufficient to highlight their message: 'Applying Human Knowledge to Improve Machine Recognition of Confusing Handwritten Numerals'.

Figure 21
Letterforms and numerals recommended by the DPB for use by dentists when filling in forms.

When Fernand Baudin (in this volume) asks us to consider what use a computer is without its memory, he refers to the traditional repertoire of typograhic knowledge. When this concept is extended to human memory, it must include the very personal and different ways that our minds may categorize or perceive any aspect of the printed character. Why should we expect the computer to mimic the human brain with its capacity for lateral thinking, its random and unpredictable reaction to any particular situation? Our perception is influenced by a lifetime of experience and emotions. Should we not instead make a virtue of the differences and use each, whether separately or together, as they work best? We should not become reliant on what is at present perhaps impossible, but may be also undesirable, or we could end by being limited by the computer instead of being liberated by it.

References

Gill E. (1931). *An Essay on Typography*. The Procrustean Bed, Chapter VI pp 91/92.

Hartley and Burnhill (1971). Experiments With Unjustified Text. *Visible Language* V 3 Summer. pp. 265-78

Nadal and Suen (1991). *Applying Human Knowledge to Improve Machine Recognition of Confusing Handwritten Numerals*. In Abstracts of papers for the Fifth Handwriting Conference of the International Graphonomics Society. pp 207-09. (Final paper in preparation).

Ovink G.W. (1938). *Legibility, Atmosphere Values and Forms of Printing Types*. Sijthoff's Uit Geversmaatschappij N.V. Leiden.

Raban B (1984). *Survey of Teachers' Opinions: Children's Books and Handwriting Styles*. In Dennis D. (ed) Reading: *Meeting Children's Special Needs*. Heinemann Educational Books.

Sassoon R. (1983). *The Practical Guide to Children's Handwriting*. Thames and Hudson.

Sassoon R. (1990). *Handwriting a New Perspective*. Stanley Thornes.

Sassoon R. (1990). *Handwriting: the Way to Teach It*. Stanley Thornes.

Schonell F.J and Goodacre E.J. (1971). *The Psychology and Teaching of Reading*. Oliver and Boyd.

Suen C.Y. (1986). 'Human Recognition of Handprinted Characters and Distance Measurements', in *Graphonomics*. Eds. Kao, van Galen and Hoosain. North Holland.

Watts L.and Nesbit J. (1974). *Legibility in Children's Books*. A Review of Research. NFER.

Yule V. (1988). The Design of Print for Children: Sales Appeal and User Appeal, in *Reading* 22(2).

Zachrisson B. (1969). 'The Problems of Congeniality in Typography', in *Typographic Opportunities in the Computer Age*. Papers of the 11th. Congress of ATypI. pp 47-51.

Zapf H. (1987) 'A Few Notes on the Legibility of Type', in David Kindersley's *Workshop*, David Kindersley and Lida Lopes Cardozo. Staatsuitgeverij – s'Gravevenhage.

ROGER WATT

The visual analysis of pages of text

Introduction

Ever since text was first printed on paper, language has had a relationship with visual perception. This relationship has existed for many centuries during which the use that language makes of our sense of visual perception has slowly evolved. The present state of the art of printing has, however, suddenly increased the rate of change in the relationship. I type this chapter into a small computer that can sit on my lap if need be. I type it in a visual form that bears no relationship to the final visual appearance of the pages. When it is prepared for printing, choices can be made concerning how it will appear, what letterforms are used, how the lines are spaced, how the words are spaced in a line and so on. Even sitting here I can experiment with such factors by typesetting on the screen of the computer. I can readily persuade myself that some settings for word spacing and line spacing are quite hopelessly poor from the point of legibility, and that others are correspondingly good. Such experimentation was quite unthinkable until very recently, and the moment is opportune for an examination of just what the visual effects of the various possible word and line spacings are. In this paper, I describe a little of visual perception, a little of typography, and then describe some formal experiments into the relationship between the two.

Vision

The purpose of vision is to take information in from the environment, to process it and to make it available for any actions or decisions that can be made However, this is a tall order, and without the appropriate expectations of what might exist in the field of view, our vision would be unable to work effectively. Our vision has specifically evolved to allow us to see the kinds of things that exist in our environment that we need to and are able to interact with. Vision is not a general purpose information gathering system, despite our confidence that it is. The difficulty that vehicle drivers can experience trying to read the road ahead when it is wet and reflecting a large number of different coloured lights is an instance of the way in which our vision can be shown to be ill-adapted to some tasks that we would wish it to perform. This same sort of difficulty can be seen when attempting to extract a phone number from a telephone directory, when a finger is often a necessary tool.

Our visual system has three important expectations of what it is likely to be presented with. First, it expects that events in the world that are very closely related will lie in adjacent parts of the image formed by the eye. For example, all the parts of a tree are very likely to lie close together. The more closely related two events are, the more close they will tend to lie to each other. Second, it expects that where there is fine scale detail, the detail will cluster together into larger units that can be used to provide a framework within which the detail can be placed. For example, the leaves on a tree are encompassed by the outline of the tree, which is a structure that doesn't actually exist. The third expectation that vision uses is that most things of interest come either in one part or in a set of connected parts. That a leaf belongs to a particular tree is determined by whether it is connected to that tree or not. The extent to which any input to the visual system conforms to these expectations will determine the ease, reliability and speed with which the visual system can analyze that input to extract the important information.

Information is present in the optical input, but not in a useful form. Vision is needed to convert the information present into a useful form. Generally, information is useful when it is explicit, not when that information is only implicit. There is information in the optical image formed by the eye about the words on a page and their order, but it is only implicitly present. At the level of the optical image, the information is represented as an array of points, each of which having a particular value corresponding to the light intensity at that point. The representation can be thought of as a matrix of numbers with each number describing the amount of light in the image at that point. An example of a matrix of numbers is given in the first figure. The numbers in this matrix represent all that can be said about the image at this stage of processing.

These values of light intensities and wavelengths at individual points in the image are the only information that is explicit in the optical image, and it is of no direct use knowing or being able to measure that the brightness of the image at such-and-such a place is a particular value.

Everything of interest in the image is determined by the patterns of light intensities in the image, by patterns in the distribution of numbers in the optical image. If we take the printed page as an example input, then this is made up of dark ink strokes on a light page surface. The initial representation of the image will only make explicit the brightnesses corresponding to the light page and the dark ink. We can imagine a different representation in which the strokes are made explicit. Imagine a list of all the strokes, each stroke being described by giving its length, width, location and so on. This list makes explicit information about the strokes. Further suitable operations performed on this list can lead to a stage where what the words are, and their order, is made explicit.

Suitable processing of the optical image needs to be used to make patterns explicit. It is helpful to think of there being two broadly different classes of visual processing operations. The first class involves operations on the light intensity array to make a new array of values, each value related to the values at and around the same place in the light intensity array. The consequence of this class of visual operations is still basically an image but with new actual values in it. The values that are calculated still make little explicit about the structure of the image. The only information

FIGURE 1
A small section of a piece of image is shown, but as a matrix of numbers rather than as a picture. Each number represents the light intensity at the corresponding place in the image. The representation only makes explicit each number, individually. Any property of the image which requires calculation rather than just reading out a number, especially the combination of more than one such number, has not been made explicit in this representation.

```
2 2 2 2 3 2 3 2 2 2 2 2 2 3 2 3 3 3 3 3 2 3 2 2 3 2 3 3 3 3 3 3 2 2 2 2 3 2 2
3 2 3 3 3 1 2 3 2 2 1 3 2 2 3 2 2 2 2 2 2 2 2 3 2 2 1 2 3 2 3 2 3 2 2 2 2 2 3 1
3 2 3 3 3 2 3 3 2 2 2 3 3 2 2 3 2 3 2 3 2 3 2 2 3 3 3 3 2 2 2 2 3 3 2 3 2 2 2 2
2 3 3 2 2 2 2 2 2 2 3 3 2 3 2 3 2 3 2 3 3 2 2 3 2 2 2 2 2 2 3 2 2 1 3 2 2 3 2
2 3 2 2 3 3 3 3 2 2 2 3 3 2 2 3 2 2 2 3 2 2 2 3 2 2 2 2 2 3 3 2 3 2 2 3 2 3
3 3 2 2 2 7 7 6 6 6 6 7 2 2 6 7 6 6 6 7 6 3 3 2 7 6 7 7 6 6 3 3 7 6 7 6 6 6 6 2 2
3 2 2 3 2 3 3 2 6 2 1 2 1 3 7 3 3 3 1 2 2 2 2 6 1 3 3 3 3 2 2 2 3 3 2 6 2 2 1 3 3
2 1 3 3 2 2 3 3 2 7 3 2 1 3 7 3 3 3 2 2 3 1 3 6 2 2 1 2 2 2 2 3 2 3 3 7 3 2 1 2 3
2 2 3 1 3 3 3 3 2 7 3 2 3 2 1 6 7 6 7 6 3 2 2 2 2 6 6 6 7 7 3 2 3 3 3 3 2 7 2 2 2 2 1
2 2 2 2 2 2 2 3 6 2 2 3 3 2 6 2 2 2 3 2 2 2 3 2 2 2 2 2 3 6 3 2 3 2 2 2 2 2 2
2 3 2 3 3 2 2 2 3 6 3 3 2 3 3 7 2 2 2 2 2 3 2 2 3 3 3 3 3 2 7 3 3 3 2 2 7 2 2 3 3 3
2 2 3 3 3 3 3 3 2 6 1 1 2 3 2 7 6 6 7 6 7 7 2 3 7 6 7 6 7 7 3 3 3 2 2 7 2 2 3 3 3
2 2 3 3 3 3 3 2 2 2 3 3 3 3 2 3 1 2 2 2 2 2 2 2 3 3 2 2 3 2 3 2 3 3 3 3 3 2 3 2 3
2 3 1 2 2 1 2 3 3 3 3 3 3 3 1 3 3 3 2 1 2 3 2 2 2 1 2 3 2 2 3 3 2 2 1 3 2 3 2
2 2 1 1 3 2 3 2 2 3 3 2 3 3 2 3 3 3 3 1 3 3 3 2 3 1 3 3 3 3 2 3 2 2 2 2 3 2 2 2 3 1
2 3 2 3 3 2 2 3 2 3 2 3 2 2 3 2 3 3 3 2 3 2 3 2 3 2 3 3 3 3 3 3 2 1 2 3 3 3 2 3 3 2
```

that is explicit is that which can be obtained by accessing individual values. The second figure shows an example of the results of applying a differentiation operation to the image piece from Figure 1. This operation makes explicit the rate of change of light intensity at each place in the image. It is a very useful operation because it removes the effects of how the image is illuminated, and because it locates the place where the image changes intensity most rapidly and which are most interesting in general.

The second class of visual processing operation is concerned with making and using descriptions of the image. A description is an alternative form of representation, which makes explicit relationships between values in the image. It is convenient to use a quasi-linguistic method of dealing with descriptions. We can express the information that a description contains by the use of a set of propositions about the image. Simple descriptions would involve the use of terms like colour, brightness, edges and lines, local motion and so on. More complex descriptions can be made from these simple ones, and might involve terms like face, surface, object and so on. It is at this descriptive stage that useful information becomes explicitly available, and the terms of the description determine how it does so. A more detailed examination of visual descriptions can be found in Watt (1991).

An important aspect of vision for what follows is the concept of spatial scale. A broad review of this topic may be found in Watt (1988). It is mistaken to think of vision as working always at the fine level of resolution that we seem to experience. For a great many purposes, a much coarser resolution is more appropriate, and finer resolutions merely add unnecessary and perhaps distracting

FIGURE 2
The same piece of image as Figure 1 is shown after the operation of differentiation has been applied to it. As before, the values are shown as a matrix of numbers. It can be seen by inspection that the non-zero values are the most important. As an image, the individual values are still all that is made explicit in this representation of the image.

```
 0  0  0  0  1 -1  1  0  0  0  0  0  0  0  1  0  0  0  0  0  1 -1  0  0  0  1  0  0  0  0  0  0  0  0  0  0  0  0  0  1  0  0
 0  0  0  0  1 -1  0  0  0  1 -1  1  0 -1  0  1  0 -1  0 -1  0  0  0  0  1  0  0  0 -1  0  0  0 -1  0  0  0  0  0  0  1 -1
 1 -1  0  0  0  0  1  0  0 -1  0  0  0  0  0 -1  0  0 -1  1  0  0  0  0  1  0 -1  0  0  1  0  0  0  0  1 -1  0  0
 0  0  0  0  0  0 -1  0  0 -1  1  0  0  0 -1  1  0  0  0  0  0  0  0  0  0 -1  0  0  0  0  0  0  0 -1  0 -1  1 -1  0  0  0
-1  0 -1  0  0  0 -1 -1  0 -1 -1 -2 -1  0 -1 -2 -1 -2 -1 -1  0 -1  0  0  0 -1 -1 -1 -1 -1 -1  0  0 -1 -1 -1 -1 -1 -1  0  0  1
 1  0  0  0  0 -1  3  2  1  2  2  2  3  0 -1  2  3  2  2  2  3  2  0  1 -1  3  2  3  2  2  3  0  0  3  1  3  2  2  2  3 -1 -1
 0  0  0  0  0  0 -1 -1 -2  1 -2 -2 -1 -1 -1  3 -2 -1 -1 -2 -1 -1 -1 -2  2 -2  0 -1 -1  0 -1 -1 -1 -1 -3  1 -2 -1 -1  0  1
 0 -1  1  0  0 -1  0  0 -1  3 -1  0  0  0  1  2 -2 -1 -1 -1  0  1 -1  0  2 -1 -1 -1 -2 -1 -1 -1  0  0  0 -1  2 -1  0  0  0
 0  0  0 -1  1  0  1  0 -2  2 -1  0  0 -2  2  2  2  2  3  0  0  0 -1 -2  3  2  2  3  2 -1 -1  0  0  0 -1  2  2  0  0  0  0
 0  0  0  0 -1  0  0 -1 -1  2 -2  0  0  0 -1  1 -2 -1 -2  0 -1  0  0  1  0 -1 -1 -1 -1 -1 -2  2  0 -1  0 -1  2 -2 -1  0  0  1
 0  0  0  0  1 -1  0  0 -1  2  0  1  0  0 -1  2 -1 -1 -1 -1 -1 -1 -1 -1  0 -1 -1 -1 -2  3 -1  0  1  0 -1 -2  3 -1 -1  0  0  1
 0  0  0  0  0  0  0  0 -1  2 -2 -1  0  1 -1  3  1  2  3  2  3  3 -1  0  3  2  2  1  3  3 -1  0  0  0 -1 -1  3  0  0  0 -1  0
 0  0  1  0  0  0  0 -1  0 -1  0  0  0 -1  0 -2 -1 -1 -1 -1  0 -1 -1 -2  0 -2 -1  0  0  0  1  0  0  0  1  0 -1  0 -1  0  0  0
 0  1 -1  0  0 -1  0  1  0  0  0  0  0  1  0 -1  0  0  0  1  0  0  0  0  1 -1  0  1  0  0  0 -1 -1  0 -1  0  0  0  0
 0 -1  1  0  0  0  0 -1  0  0  0  0  0  0  0  0 -1  0  1  0  1  0 -1  0  0 -1  0  0  0  0  1  0  0  1  0  0  1 -1  1  0
 0  0 -1 -1  1  0  0  0  0  0  0 -1  0  0 -1  0  0  0 -1  1  0  0 -1  1 -1  0  0  0  0 -1  0  0  0  0  0  0  0 -1  0 -1
 0  0  0  0  0 -1  0  0  0  0  0  0  0  0  0  0  0 -1  0  0  0 -1  0  0 -1  1 -1  0  0 -1  0  0  0  0  0  0 -1  1  0  0
```

detail. The shape of a tree is much better specified at a relatively coarse level of resolution. In practice, the visual system generates a number of different versions of any image that is presented to it, spanning the useful range of resolutions. Each one is created from the original image by a process that is analogous to blurring. The different degrees of blurring make different structures within the image available for further analysis and description. There is evidence that even when the finer details are necessary they are analyzed by human vision only after it has used the coarse levels of resolution to build a framework into which they may be placed (Watt 1987). It is thought that this reflects a fundamental difficulty in processing the exact location of things within the visual field (Watt 1990). If this is true, then the reading of text, which must depend critically on the ability of the visual system to calculate correctly the relative positions of letters and words, must also depend on the appropriate use of spatial scale. Some examples of text as seen at different resolutions or spatial scales is shown below.

Typography
Typography is concerned with the transmission of linguistic material through the medium of visual pattern. Traditionally, the pattern was printed or written on paper; more recently, it is likely that the pattern will be presented on a visual display device. The quality of most visual displays is not yet sufficiently high for much of the knowledge and experience of typography to be applied, although that situation may change in the near future. A linguistic message is passed from its author to a receiver by being printed, that is, by being coded as a series of dark marks on a white piece of paper. These ink marks are laid out in a systematic pattern and according to a set of general rules that conform to the reader's expectations and capabilities. There is no logical reason why the letters of a word, or the strokes of a letter for that matter, should be kept in close spatial proximity. For example, the sentence

      Mary had a little lamb

can also be printed as

      Mhall aa_ia rd_tm y_ _tb _ _ _l_ _ _ _e_

without any loss of information (the first group of letters contains the first letter of each word in order; the second group the second letters and so on). However, there is an obvious loss of readability. This loss of readability is presumably based on two different factors. Obviously, unless the reader knows the convention for placing the letters, then no sense can be made of the material without a great deal of effort. More subtly, but more importantly, the material is also difficult to read because it does not conform to the ways in which our visual system can take in information. It can only partly be due to the fact that we have not been trained to read a language that is presented in this way, and is mostly due to the fact that our visual system habitually takes in information in a fashion that makes the first layout very much better. We are so accumstomed to seeing text printed in what seems a commonsense way that we tend to lose sight of the fact that in a purely logical sense it is arbitrary: any other systematic layout would suffice the information/communication demands equally well.

For a visual system, the layout of text in a paragraph is not in the least bit arbitrary, but must rather conform to the manner in which that visual system is able to process the information. The ways in which our vision is able to process input is determined by its requirement to produce a fast response to the contents of natural scenes. When we use our sense of vision to take in linguistic material, we are using a system that was designed to do something very different. The characteristics of the receiver system are fixed and so the characteristics of the transmission itself must be adjusted to match as closely as possible.

It is quite apparent that we cannot read a whole page in one go: we have to scan the page in sequence. This is primarily because the quality of our vision deteriorates towards the periphery of our visual field. Clearly the material should be laid out on the page so as to minimize the amount of scanning that is required. It is sensible to place the information about words in the sequence in which they were produced or would be spoken. This means that it is sensible to place all the information about a single word in as near to a single location as can be achieved. It is also necessary to clearly demark that information by surrounding it by an area of white space, because our visual system expects objects, single entities, to be distinct from their surrounds. Given this, the overall layout of words in a paragraph of text makes simple sense, but does

Eversincetextwasfirstprintedonpaper, languagehashadarelationship
withvisualperception. Thisrelationshiphasnowexistedformanycenturie
overwhichtheusethatlanguagemakesofoursenseofvisualperceptionhas
slowlyevolved. Thepresentstateoftheartofprintinghashowever, suddc
increasedtherateofchangeintherelationship. Itypethischapterintoa
smallcomputerthatcansitonmylapifneedbe. Itypeitinaformthat
bearsnorelationshiptothefinalvisualappearanceofthepages. Whenitis
preparedforprinting, choicescanbemadeconcerninghowitwillappear,
letterformsareused, howthelinesarespaced, howthewordsarespacedir
lineandsoon. EvensittinghereIcanexperimentwithsuchfactorsby
typesettingonthescreenofthecomputer. Icanreadilypersuademyselfthat
somesettingsforwordspacingandlinespacingarequitehopelesslypoorfror
thepointoflegibility, andthatothersarecorrespondinglygood. Such
experimentationhasbeenquiteunthinkableuntilveryrecently, andthemon
isopportuneforanexaminationofjustwhatthevisualeffectsofthevarious
possiblewordandlinespacingsare. Inthispaper, Idescribealittleof

Ever since text was first printed on paper, language has had a relati
with visual perception. This relationship has now existed for many
over which the use that language makes of our sense of visual perce
slowly evolved. The present state of the art of printing has howevei
increased the rate of change in the relationship. I type this chapter in
small computer that can sit on my lap if need be. I type it in a form
bears no relationship to the final visual appearance of the pages. WI
prepared for printing, choices can be made concerning how it will a
letter forms are used, how the lines are spaced, how the words are
line and so on. Even sitting here I can experiment with such factors
typesetting on the screen of the computer. I can readily persuade m
some settings for word spacing and line spacing are quite hopelessly
the point of legibility, and that others are correspondingly good. Si
experimentation has been quite unthinkable until very recently, and
is opportune for an examination of just what the visual effects of the
possible word and line spacings are. In this paper, I describe a littl

Eversincetextwasfirstprintedonpaper,languagehashadarelationship
withvisualperception. Thisrelationshiphasnowexistedformanycenturies
overwhichtheusethatlanguagemakesofoursenseofvisualperceptionhas
slowlyevolved. Thepresentstateoftheartofprintinghashowever,suddenly
increasedtherateofchangeintherelationship. Itypethischapterintoa
smallcomputerthatcansitonmylapifneedbe. Itypeitinaformthat
bearsnorelationshiptothefinalvisualappearanceofthepages. Whenitis
preparedforprinting,choicescanbemadeconcerninghowitwillappear,what
letterformsareused,howthelinesarespaced,howthewordsarespacedina
lineandsoon. EvensittinghereIcanexperimentwithsuchfactorsby
typesettingonthescreenofthecomputer. Icanreadilypersuademyselfthat
somesettingsforwordspacingandlinespacingarequitehopelesslypoorfrom
thepointoflegibility,andthatothersarecorrespondinglygood. Such
experimentationhasbeenquiteunthinkableuntilveryrecently,andthemoment
isopportuneforanexaminationofjustwhatthevisualeffectsofthevarious
possiblewordandlinespacingsare. Inthispaper,Idescribealittleof
typography,alittleofvisualperception,andthendescribesomeformal
experimentsintotherelationshipbetweenthetwo.

Ever since text was first printed on paper, language has had a relationship
with visual perception. This relationship has now existed for many centurie
over which the use that language makes of our sense of visual perception h;
slowly evolved. The present state of the art of printing has however, sudde
increased the rate of change in the relationship. I type this chapter into a
small computer that can sit on my lap if need be. I type it in a form that
bears no relationship to the final visual appearance of the pages. When it is
prepared for printing, choices can be made concerning how it will appear, v
letter forms are used, how the lines are spaced, how the words are spaced i
line and so on. Even sitting here I can experiment with such factors by
typesetting on the screen of the computer. I can readily persuade myself tha
some settings for word spacing and line spacing are quite hopelessly poor fi
the point of legibility, and that others are correspondingly good. Such
experimentation has been quite unthinkable until very recently, and the mom
is opportune for an examination of just what the visual effects of the variou:
possible word and line spacings are. In this paper, I describe a little of
typography, a little of visual perception, and then describe some formal
experiments into the relationship between the two.

Ever since text was first printed on paper, language has had
with visual perception. This relationship has now existed for
over which the use that language makes of our sense of vis
slowly evolved. The present state of the art of printing has
increased the rate of change in the relationship. I type this c
small computer that can sit on my lap if need be. I type it
bears no relationship to the final visual appearance of the pa
prepared for printing, choices can be made concerning how it
letter forms are used, how the lines are spaced, how the w
line and so on. Even sitting here I can experiment with suc
typesetting on the screen of the computer. I can readily pers
some settings for word spacing and line spacing are quite h
the point of legibility, and that others are correspondingly go
experimentation has been quite unthinkable until very recently,
is opportune for an examination of just what the visual effec
possible word and line spacings are. In this paper, I describ

Ever since text was first printed on paper, language has had a rela
with visual perception. This relationship has now existed for many
over which the use that language makes of our sense of visual per
slowly evolved. The present state of the art of printing has howeve
increased the rate of change in the relationship. I type this chapter
small computer that can sit on my lap if need be. I type it in a
bears no relationship to the final visual appearance of the pages. W
prepared for printing, choices can be made concerning how it will
letter forms are used, how the lines are spaced, how the words an
line and so on. Even sitting here I can experiment with such facto
typesetting on the screen of the computer. I can readily persuade m
some settings for word spacing and line spacing are quite hopelessl
the point of legibility, and that others are correspondingly good. Su
experimentation has been quite unthinkable until very recently, and tl
is opportune for an examination of just what the visual effects of
possible word and line spacings are. In this paper, I describe a litt
typography, a little of visual perception, and then describe some for
experiments into the relationship between the two.

FIGURE 3
This figure shows nine examples of how text could be
laid out on paper. The examples differ in two
dimensions, the inter-word spacing and the inter-line
spacing. The central version is the closest to good layout,
and each of the others is less good in some way.

leave several quantitative aspects of the paragraph design open. How much space should be left around each word? Obviously a word should be closer to the words that immediately precede and follow it in the narrative. In the third figure, a small section of a narrative is printed with a variety of different spacings, horizontally between words, and vertically between lines, to illustrate the different effects that can be obtained by varying such parameters.

Looking at the examples shown in Figure 3, typographers will see cases that are just bad practice, cases that are acceptable, but expensive because they do not fit a sufficiently high number of words into a page, and some cases that would represent good practice. Good practice has largely evolved, as do most design processes, by trial, error and aesthetic judgement. There is nothing wrong with this, but it is of some interest to discover whether there is some real visual basis in readability. The main thrust of the rest of this paper is to argue that there is such a basis.

Computational analysis
In this section, an analysis of paragraphs of text is described. The analysis concerns a variety of different layouts of text in a single paragraph, differing in how the white space is used: the samples in Figure 3 span the range of variations that have been considered. The analysis comprises several steps. First, samples of text are created. Next the samples are digitized either from a bitmap, or by using a scanner and hard copy. The resultant digital images are processed, as will be described, to produce a desciption of the structure of the image. This processing is a close analogy of the actual sequence of operations performed by human vision. Visual inspection has identified several parts of the resultant description that correspond to visual features that are obviously of use in reading and scanning a paragraph of text. The fate of these parts of the description as typographical variables are altered is then considered.

It is necessary to give some details of the image processing techniques that were applied to paragraphs of text, before describing the results of having done so.

Text generation
The general style is roughly equivalent to standard practice: each character occupies a logical rectangle, each edge of which it

touches somewhere. Space between characters is then created by placing them to a precision of 1 point. Apple TrueType and Postscript 'Times' font was used. Hard copy was generated on an Apple LaserWriter at 300dpi. A typical digitized image of text generated in this way is shown in Figure 4.

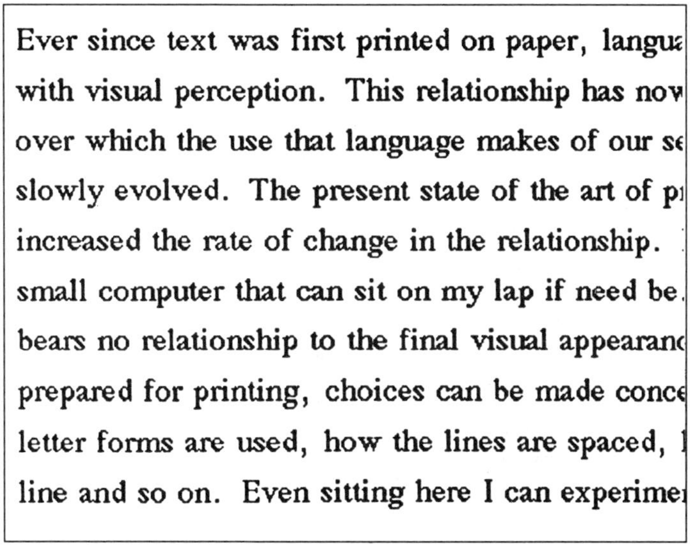

Ever since text was first printed on paper, langua
with visual perception. This relationship has nov
over which the use that language makes of our se
slowly evolved. The present state of the art of pi
increased the rate of change in the relationship.
small computer that can sit on my lap if need be.
bears no relationship to the final visual appearanc
prepared for printing, choices can be made conce
letter forms are used, how the lines are spaced, l
line and so on. Even sitting here I can experimei

FIGURE 4
This figure shows the digitized version of a sample image that was generated as described in the text. The quality is relatively poor, for a hard copy version because resolution is set to 72 dpi.

Image processing technique

The sequence of operations applied is one which can be viewed as representing a conservative approach to the issues of what human vision actually does (see Watt 1990). There is considerable debate yet about the details of the process of human vision. The technique that I have applied here is one that can be taken as representing the commonality of the various models that have been proposed. The software that was used forms part of a general purpose vision system that has been developed at Stirling University. It runs under Unix, is written in C, and is available with documentation upon request.

There are two basic steps in the processing of an image. First the image is filtered with the Laplacian of a Gaussian. The Gaussian simply blurs the image out equally in all directions. The Laplacian replaces an image by one in which the rate of change of intensity is recorded. In this process, there is a single free parameter, which is the size of the Gaussian. This free parameter is described as the spatial scale of analysis. The result of applying this operation to any image is a new image, parts of which have positive values and parts of which have negative ones. The values tend to cluster into regions all of which are either positive or negative. Each of these regions is called a blob.

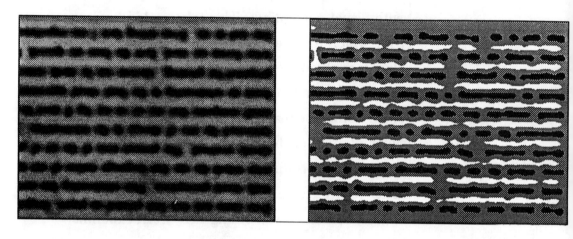

The second stage of the processing is to create a description of each blob. The description is a list of parameters, each one describing some aspect of the blob. In the work described here, there are three parameters of interest. Each blob has a mass which is simply the total sum of all the pixel values within the blob boundary: a large mass could reflect either a large area or a particularly strong amplitude of response, or both. Most blobs that are found, irrespective of the source of the original image, are somewhat elongated and this elongation can be given an orientation and a length. The orientation is calculated by finding the line which, when drawn through the blob, causes the sum of the squared deviations of the blob to be at its smallest value. This line is known as the principal axis. The length is calculated by finding the standard deviation of the blob along the direction of the blob orientation.

For any particular image, filtered at any particular spatial scale, a set of blobs can be found. For each of these blobs, a description is

FIGURE 5
The image of Figure 4 is shown on the left after filtering with a Laplacian of a Gaussian. The Gaussian has a relatively large width, giving quite a coarse spatial scale. On the right is shown the same image, but with the blobs emphasized slightly. Notice how the blobs correspond to a smoothed version of the original.

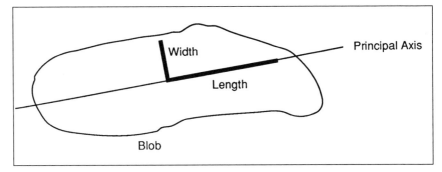

FIGURE 6
A blob and its description are shown. The thin line through the blob represents where the principal axis of the blob lies. The angle that this axis makes with the horizontal, measured anti-clockwise, is the orientation of the blob. The blob has a length that is given by its standard deviation in the direction of the axis.

created, and so for the filtered image there is a set of blob descriptions. This complete set is a description of the filtered image. For present purposes, the set is then summarized by drawing two histograms showing the distributions of mass at different lengths and orientations. Each blob is taken, and its mass is added to the length histogram at the point corresponding to the length of the blob, and its mass is added to the orientation histogram at the point corresponding to the orientation of the blob. By repeating this for all the blobs in a particular filtered image, the two histograms can be created. Example histograms are shown in the figure. Each histogram is actually a pair because it is important, as will be seen, to keep the dark blobs and the light blobs separate.

FIGURE 7
The two histograms in this figure show how the mass in the previous filtered image is distributed amongst blobs of different lengths and orientations.

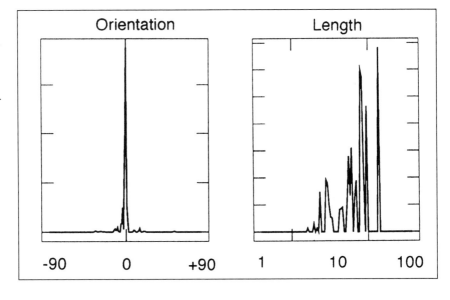

The calculation of the two histograms, for length and for orientation, can be repeated at many different spatial scales so that a pair of more complex histograms can be produced showing how the distribution of mass at different lengths and orientations varies with spatial scale. These latter histograms provide the basis for the analysis that I now describe. In all of these histograms the negative blobs and the positive blobs are treated quite separately.

Thus an image showing a sample of text, laid out according to certain values of the typographical variables of interest, is processed to produce a pair of complex histograms. These histograms are themselves just matrices of numbers, the same form as the original image, but now the values within correspond to very different aspects of the text. This is a representation of the image that has been used for the purposes of texture analysis (Watt 1992).

FIGURE 8
This figure shows the final representation of the original digitized image. The histograms are shown as density plots, so that the darker the picture, the greater the amount of mass at that point in the histogram. At the fine resolution in scale, length and orientation, individual blobs can be tracked through the plots. Notice that logarithmic scales are used for spatial scale and for length.

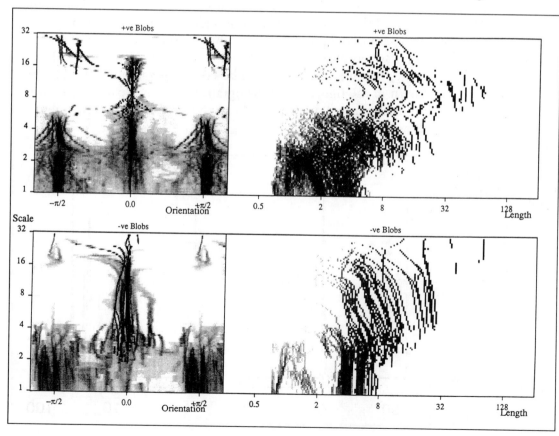

Observations

I start describing the main observations of this study by examining
the histograms of length and orientation as functions of spatial
scale. To start with we are only interested in whether there is any
identifiable pattern in these histograms, and not with what aspects
of the paragraph of text the pattern might correspond to. Figure 8
shows the histograms that result for the sample of text shown in a
Figure 4. This sample is the closest to conventional typography, is
apparently the easiest to read, and will be considered first.

The first and most important observation is that there is a striking
pattern in the resultant histograms. Examining the orientation
histograms, it can be seen that there are three distinct bands, with
relatively sharp boundaries between:

1)   At the finest scales, most of the blobs are vertical or near
     vertical.

2)   At intermediate scales, the blobs are all aligned at or near the
     horizontal.

3)   At the coarsest scales, the orientation of the blobs is much
     less organized, although there is an overall predominance of
     vertical blobs in the light histograms and a predominance of
     horizontals in the dark histograms.

In the example shown there is a fourth region that can only be
seen by examining the differences between the positive blobs and
the negative blobs. The actual scale at which the intermediate scale
horizontal blobs switch to the finer scale vertical blobs is different
in the two histograms.

4)   There is a fourth region in which the positive blobs are
     predominantly vertical and the negative blobs are
     predominantly horizontal.

The general pattern of the first three bands has occurred in every
sample of normal text that has been examined in this way. The
fourth band in the histograms has been found in many, but not all,
samples of text. There are echoes of this same organization into
distinctive bands of spatial scale, when we examine the length

histograms. Although the bands are less clearly marked, they are, nonetheless of the same general set:

1)   At the finest scales, the lengths are all short, as would be expected. Over this range of scales, however, there are two interesting features in the dark histogram. First, the lengths do not change markedly with increasing spatial scale, and second, the length distributions is clearly bimodal.

2)   There is then a relatively sudden change in the range of blob lengths that are seen as we move into the next range of spatial scales. The blobs are now both much longer and span a wider range. In this range of scales, the dark blobs are clustered into discrete lengths, rather than following a relatively smooth distribution.

3)   At coarse scales, there are two features of note. The dark blobs tend to be very long. The bright blobs switch from being very long to being much shorter in length as the spatial scale is increased still further.

Overall, the following structures can be identified. At fine scales (approx. 1 − 3) there are short vertical blobs, dark and light. The dark blobs tend to be distributed between two lengths. The bright blobs show a reduction in length as scale is increased (from 1 to 2). At the next more coarse range of scales (approx. 3 − 6) there are significant structures in the bright histograms. The blobs are vertical and have a length that is about the same as that for the longer dark blobs in the finest scales. In this range of scales the dark blobs increase rapidly in length, but are all horizontal, unlike the bright blobs. At the third range of scales (approx. 6 − 16) the blobs are all horizontal, with a characteristically discrete distribution of dark blob lengths, and extremely long bright blobs. The final structures are found at the coarsest scales (approx 16 − 32). These are bright blobs that are shorter in length than those in the previous band, and are vertical not horizontal.

Interpretation
Now we can turn to the question of how to interpret the structures that have been described. The easiest way to do this is to

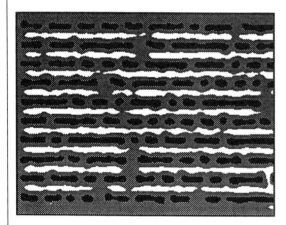

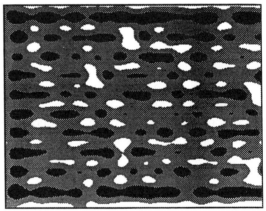

FIGURE 9
The sample of text from figure 4 is shown after filtering. Four scales are shown, selected to show the different organizations that can be found.

take a sample paragraph of text and display it after processing at each of the four basic ranges of spatial scale. These are shown in Figure 9.

Although not very obvious, at the coarsest scale, the bright blobs correspond to the locations of major features such as sentence breaks and rivers in the text. At the next level of scale down, the blobs which are all horizontal, correspond most closely to the line structure in the text, with dark blobs lining along the words (but not necessarily in a one-to-one correspondence with them) and the bright blobs lining up in the inter-line space, possibly extending across the whole paragraph. The next scale is the most interesting, being that scale where the bright blobs are mostly vertical and the dark blobs are mostly horizontal. In this scale the dark blobs are registering whole-word structure. The bright blobs are of two different types, the most visible ones being in a one-to-one relationship with word breaks, so that every vertical bright blob marks a gap between two words, and every gap between two words is marked by one of these blobs. In addition to this, however, there are some much smaller bright blobs that are aligned at the ends of ascenders or descenders. At the finest scale, the blobs are all related to letter level structures. The bright blobs represent the space between strokes. The dark blobs are predominantly the heavier vertical strokes of letters. These come in two lengths corresponding to ordinary letters and taller letters.

Typographical effects

The same analysis has been applied to various combinations of the two main typographical parameters that are being considered here, namely word and line spacing. Some sample histogram representations are shown in Figure 10. Each one is derived from the corresponding sample of text in Figure 3. As before, the central one can be taken as nearly ideal.

The first important observation is that the effects of word and of line spacing are not separable. Inspection of the histograms to find which combinations of word and line spacing alter any of the features shows that the effects of word spacing depend on line spacing and vice versa.

For the analysis that has been carried out here, the features in the histograms that are associated with letter level characteristics are not noticeably affected by word or line spacing. This is not unexpected. The features that correspond to the characteristics of larger levels in the text do depend in every case on line and word spacing.

At the word level, the basic features are the dark horizontal blobs corresponding to the words themselves and the vertical light blobs corresponding to the word breaks. If the word spacing is too close and if the line spacing is too close, irrespective of the word spacing, then the dark word blobs are lost. Similarly if the word spacing is too close, then the light blobs corresponding to word breaks are lost. These features are also lost if the word spacing is too large. If the line spacing is too close, then, depending on the word spacing, the word breaks may become merged vertically between lines to create rivers even at this relatively fine scale.

At the line level the dark blobs will switch from being due to individual words or small groups of words to being due to whole lines. This effect is exaggerated if the line spacing is too wide. A line spacing that is too wide also leads to very long horizontal light blobs between each line.

At a paragraph level, the main features of interest in the present analysis are sentence breaks and rivers. The presence or absence of sentence breaks depends on how much space is left in the break and is not markedly affected by the typographical parameters that have been considered here. The rivers are more interesting. The presence of rivers depends on having a suitable line spacing and word spacing. If the word spacing is too narrow, then the rivers are lost. For a given word spacing, it appears that the incidence of rivers depends the line spacing. If the line spacing is too wide, then the result is a total absence of any rivers, irrespective of the word spacing. If the line spacing is too narrow and the word spacing is wide, there are potentially very many rivers.

All of the observations that have been made here are provisional in that they are not based on a large sample of materials. At the very least, further analysis is necessary with variations in font and in character spacing.

Discussion

There are important points to be discussed in the light of the observations above. Before doing so, however, there are two qualifications to be made. First, the range of text materials used to establish what a 'normal' pattern might be may well be insufficient and biased. Second, it is one thing to discover what information could be available for reading after normal visual processing, it is quite another to show that it is normally used, although preliminary studies in this laboratory are proving encouraging.

The main points for further discussion concern the accessibility and utility of the patterns of response that have been identified and the extent to which they depend upon the typographical parameters that were used to lay out the paragraph.

The histogram patterns shown above are visually very striking. The rather discontinuous changes in structure between the

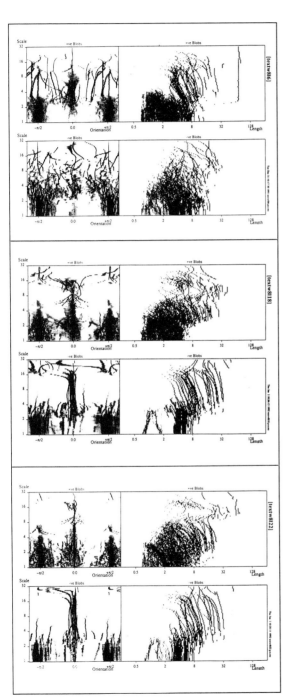

FIGURE 10
This figure shows the histogram descriptions for the samples of text shown in Figure 3. Comparing the two figures, it can be seen how the choice of typographical variable can alter the structures available in the visual response to the paragraph of text.

different important bands of spatial scale, plus the relative stability
of the structure within each band, means that a process that relied
on extracting this pattern would be quite tolerant of uncertainty or
error. This is likely to imply that the patterns are also quite easy to
extract – that they are accessible.

Reading paragraphs of text
When we read from a paragraph of text, there is a complex
information processing task going on to allow the marks of ink on
the page to be brought together and processed in appropriately
sized chunks and in an appropriate order. Seen from the point of
view of a visual system presented with a paragraph of material,
about which it has little or no information, it is possible to
understand that there are several immediate problems that need to
be solved before reading as such can take place. The first problem
is that a page of text can be viewed from any distance and the
resultant optical image that the brain has to process can be formed
at a wide range of magnifications. This magnification needs to be
measured. Then the page needs to oriented so that the lines run
horizontally, or at least the orientation of the lines needs to be
known. Beyond this, there are further pre-reading tasks that will
depend on the nature of the reading that is to be done. At this
stage it is important to be able to move the eyes around the page
to bring selected parts of it into the fine acuity vision of our central
fovea. All of the information for this pre-reading preparation must
come from a visual analysis of the page itself.

Once the page has been properly aligned and the principal
landmarks established, then it is possible to start reading. In reading
it is important to be able to take in information from the words on
the page in roughly the correct order, although some words can be
skipped altogether and others might be analyzed out of turn.
Generally, the words that can be skipped are the function words
that are typically small. Before deciding whether to read a word or
to skip it, it is therefore useful to have some information about that
word. In analyzing a word, it is important that most if not all of
the information about that word be taken, without including any
information about words nearby. Reading can be an active process
in which the reader will return to parts of the page for re-reading,
will look away for a second and then return and wish to continue.

In order to be able to continue without having to start again, it is useful to have a representation of a few landmarks in the text that can be used for navigation about the page.

Visual representations of paragraphs of text
The histograms that have been described above provide a useful representation of a paragraph of text in their own right, even though they do not of themselves allow the identification of the linguistic material. If the paragraph of text is brought closer to the eyes or taken further away, then the orientation histograms will slide vertically up or down and the length histograms will slide up and to the right or down and to the left. Given that there are some very obvious features in the histograms and places where the structure changes very radiply, the vertical location of any one histogram, and hence the magnification of the page of text, can be assessed very easily. If the page is rotated away from vertical, then the orientation histograms will simply slide horizontally (the length histograms are unchanged). Once again the exact orientation of the page of text can thus be easily obtained from the histogram representation.

Beyond this, histograms provide information about the scales of processing that have the different structures of interest. Rivers are useful landmarks for navigation, so long as there are not too many for them to become confused. The histograms make available information about the scales at which rivers are most apparent. Sentence breaks are also useful in this respect and, in general typographical practice, are most apparent at the same scales as rivers, which is an interesting coincidence. The histograms also provide information about the relevant scales for word level structures. The scales which appear to be most characteristic of word structures are scales that have a great deal of useful information.

Adjusting typography to suit vision
It is possible to reverse the examination of text that has been carried out now and investigate how typographical parameters should be set to suit vision. In this respect it is important to note that there will never be a single best layout, independent of the material and its intended function. However, by making a few

simple assumptions about the criteria that paragraph layout should meet, it is possible to see what types of consideration are most important. Two examples are given.

At coarse scales, rivers are important: too few, and the paragraph will lack in landmarks for navigation; too many, and the paragraph will have too many similar landmarks, making the finding of any particular one difficult. The number of rivers is controlled by the joint relationships of word and line spacing to the character size and to each other. For a given line spacing, and within limits, the optimum word spacing for an appropriate number of rivers can be decided.

At finer scales, word breaks are important. These are also affected by both word and line spacings, and their relationship to the character size. Once again, for a given line spacing, and within limits, the optimum word spacing for generating markers for word breaks can be decided.

It is not known with any certainty what the dependence between these two features is and how they co-depend on the choices of word and line spacing. They do illustrate, however, the possibility of being able to control the layout of text in a paragraph, not by specifying the word and line spacings directly, but by specifying the visual effect desired – the 'riveriness' and the 'wordiness' of the paragraph. Moreover, these could then be held as the size of the printed characters was varied. From the point of view of unsophisticated users of desktop publishing systems, this would allow them appropriate freedoms in paragraph design rather than the more standard freedoms of typographical parameters which may not be appropriate for those who are not experienced typographers.

Summary
A method for creating a visual description of the effect of a paragraph of text has been described. The method generates a representation of the paragraph that has certain significant patterns. Many of these patterns could be useful. At the most simple level, it could be that under certain circumstances, readers actually look for and use the features of these patterns in order to control the process of reading a page of text. It is highly likely that eye-movements, for example, are determined by the information available at the coarser scales. The fact that the pattern changes in

such a marked manner with differences in spatial scale implies that the problem of how to judge the size of letters and words could be solved without much prior knowledge about the actual instance of text, but just with some knowledge about text in general. This would be extremely useful in avoiding the so-called size-invariance problem which is concerned with knowing how to allow for the natural variations in the size of objects, including letters and words.

The pattern of structure that is shown in the histograms and in the underlying relationship between blobs and the linguistic structures in a paragraph of text is sensitive to the choice of typographical parameters. In particular, there are constraints on word spacing which must be neither too wide nor too narrow with respect to the line spacing and letter spacing, and there are constraints on the line spacing which also must be neither too wide nor too narrow. It is clearly important to discover more about the boundary conditions for this phenomenon and its relationship to both appearance and legibility.

Even if it is not the case that the human visual system habitually uses the features that have been described here, it is very plausible that these features are closely correlated with the features that it does use, and that the present patterns and structures can be taken as an indication of how good a particular set of typsetting parameters is.

Acknowledgements
The work described here was supported by the Royal Society of Edinburgh, a project grant from SERC, and ESPRIT BRA INSIGHT.

References
Watt, R.J. (1987). Scanning from coarse to fine spatial scales in the human visual system after the onset of a stimulus. J. Opt. Soc. Amer., A4, 2006-2021.

Watt, R.J. (1988). *Visual Processing: Computational, Psychophysical and Cognitive Research.* Lawrence-Erlbaum Associates, Sussex.

Watt R.J. (1990). The Primal Sketch in Human Vision. In *AI and the Eye* (Eds. A.Blake & T.Troscianko). John Wiley.

Watt, R.J. (1991). *Understanding Vision.* Academic Press, London.

Index